REDEFINING
✓POSSIBLE

REVISED AND UPDATED

REVISED AND UPDATED

Proven Strategies *to*
Break Belief Barriers *and*
Create Your New Normal

RON ALFORD

SouthwesternBooks

Copyright © 2021, 2024 Southwestern/Great American, Inc., dba Southwestern Family of Companies

All rights reserved. No part of this book may be reproduced or transmitted in any form or by any means, electronic or mechanical, including photocopying or recording, or by any information retrieval system, without the written permission of the copyright holder.

This revised and updated edition of *Redefining Possible: Proven Strategies to Break Belief Barriers and Create Your New Normal* was published by Southwestern Books. Southwestern Books is an imprint of Southwestern Publishing House, Inc., 2451 Atrium Way, Nashville, TN 37214. Southwestern Publishing House is a wholly owned subsidiary of Southwestern Family of Companies, Inc., Nashville, TN.

Published in association with Southwestern Consulting.
info@southwesternconsulting.com
southwesternconsulting.com | 615-391-2834

Southwestern Books are available at special quantity discounts for bulk purchases for sales promotions, premiums, fundraising, or educational use. Special books or book excerpts can be created to fit specific needs at the compliance of the author. For details, write sales@southwesternbooks.com.

Cover design by Kristen Ingebretson
Interior design by Vicky Shea

Scripture is taken from the Holy Bible, New Living Translation, copyright © 1996, 2004, 2015 by Tyndale House Foundation. Used by permission of Tyndale House Publishers, Inc., Carol Stream, IL 60188. All rights reserved.

ISBN: 979-8-9905615-0-2 (revised and updated edition)

Library of Congress Control Number: 2024937982

Printed in Canada

10 9 8 7 6 5 4 3 2 1

Dedication

I'd like to dedicate this book to my three kids, Van, P. K., and Hartley, and to my wife, Desireé. This book gives so much purpose to every challenge our family has faced and will face in the future, and it makes all the joys that much sweeter. You four are my biggest inspirations for all that I do. I am driven to be the best example that a man can be, to use every gift that God has given me, and to be someone you four are proud to call "Dad" and "Husband." I hope this book honors you and shows how much I love you as well as how grateful I am to God for all He has given us.

This book is also dedicated to everyone who is out there searching. I believe that God put us on the planet for a reason. Sadly, some people go their whole lives without finding their purpose. In fact, massive numbers of people know they could be getting more out of life but don't know how. This book is dedicated to those who are willing to look into the mirror and admit that they want to make changes . . . and not let where they have been hold them back. If this describes you, I invite you to read this book and redefine possible.

Contents

Foreword 9

Introduction: The Power of Possible 13

Strategy One: Sharpen Your Focus 29

Strategy Two: Own Your Past, Present, and Future 51

Strategy Three: Clarify Your Vision 71

Strategy Four: Strengthen Your Belief System 95

Strategy Five: Cultivate Confidence 115

Strategy Six: Fortify Your Faith 137

The Payoff: Prepare for Impact 159

Conclusion: Possible Doesn't Happen Alone 179

Appendix A: The RAFT™ Technique 187

Appendix B: Gratitude 195

Appendix C: The Power of Self-Talk 201

Appendix D: Strategy Tactics 207

Acknowledgments 217

Endnotes 218

About the Author 221

Foreword

Perhaps the greatest benefit of working so long with a company that attracts uniquely motivated young people, and then gives them a chance to either fall flat on their face or fly to the moon, is seeing some of them rise beyond the common and selfish quest for personal achievement and center on a mission of making the world better. Ron Alford has done just that, making a great and progressive impact on that mission by giving us *Redefining Possible*.

As the former president of Southwestern Advantage, I have known this young man since he was a college student selling educational systems door-to-door in our award-winning internship program, which was founded in 1868. Ron spent twenty years working for Southwestern Advantage and is the third-highest lifetime producer (out of 200,000 lifetime team members). In 2013, he joined Southwestern Consulting—another business within Southwestern Family of Companies—where he earned a senior partnership in record time and continues to break records as a top producer. Ron also works for Southwestern Coaching, the one-on-one coaching arm of Southwestern Consulting, where he is one of only three recipients of the company's Trifecta Award, the highest honor given to those who reach the peak of selling, recruiting, and team leadership. He has received this award a record three times.

I consider it a personal privilege to have seen Ron become a record setter and catalyst in the success of so many others. I have seen him both at work and at play. I have seen him with his family. I have seen him strive every day to live consistently well and positively impact the world. He goes about this not in a way where he gets everything right every time (no one does that), but in a way that is based on a complete lack of vanity and an immense sense of gratitude for his opportunities and abilities.

Ron has achieved a great level of professional success, yet he writes from a position of deep humility. He fearlessly reveals some of his most profound personal failures, fully accepting responsibility—and therefore speaking from places where we all can connect.

This is far from a self-help book. It's a self-realization book. The six strategies outlined here have three things in common: they are rooted in reality, they work (if we do), and they challenge us to be better at life.

As I read this book, I was expecting it to be "good," with useful information. I wasn't expecting it to get under my skin. With its powerful formula, this book can help literally anyone reach a new awareness of what they can accomplish and, more important, why they should strive to redefine possible.

There are books about focus, and there are books about taking ownership. Yet in a lightbulb moment, Ron has combined these strategies powerfully to create a lifelong, sustainable vision to accomplish more and live with greater purpose. This in turn creates a unique and comprehensive synergy of forces and abilities.

There are also books about increasing belief and books about gaining more confidence. Yet in combining those actions with faith as the result, the author has caused me to think differently about faith in my daily pursuits (apart from any religious connotations).

The most powerful formula is at the end of the book. When combining all six strategies, the result is impact—transforming the lives of others for the better. Impact is the outgrowth of these powerful strategies, the payoff for all the hard work of *redefining*. In fact, the author suggests that impact is the purpose of this life.

Most significant to me personally is the concept in chapter 5 called "confidence anchors." All people have wins, and all people have losses. Too often, we dwell repeatedly on our losses, and we tend to put less emphasis on our wins. As Ron says, "We experience storms all day, every day. That's why we need confidence anchors." A confidence anchor is "a victory that you can revisit—a memory of a time when you redefined what was possible." Everyone has had at least one of those times. By nurturing that memory, we can create a stepping-stone to another moment of redefinition. Ron wisely admonishes us to avoid complacency in this process, because "as soon as you've peaked, everything else is downhill."

Ron has been a frequent speaker and coach to the Southwestern Advantage team members and independent educational system dealers. His underlying message—that "possible" is up to us—has helped us to fuel our own redefinition at Southwestern Advantage.

Our dedicated team has employed every one of the six strategies in this book, and we have succeeded in redefining possible.

Ron Alford spent more than three years working specifically on this book and decades studying, learning, and living out the content. He has used the principles in this book in many different ways and become stronger for it—from navigating unprecedented external circumstances, like leading Southwestern Consulting through the beginning of the pandemic in 2020–2021, to successfully overcoming his own deep personal challenges. That's why this book is so important—why this is a book for our times. When the hope-poisoning word *impossible* can easily become a collective mindset, a potent antidote must be readily at hand.

Redefining Possible is that antidote.

Dan Moore
Former President, Southwestern Advantage
April 2024

[INTRODUCTION]

The Power of Possible

It was March 2020, and Southwestern Consulting was on the precipice of reaching a new high. As one of the world's fastest-growing sales and leadership coaching, keynote speaking, and consulting organizations, the company was growing year over year and was positioned to increase revenue by 15 percent from 2019 to 2020. Around the world, more than one hundred certified coaches were growing their business and achieving their goals. All signs pointed toward even more explosive growth in the year to come.

Then, faster than anyone could have imagined, everything changed with the COVID-19 pandemic and the global state of emergency. The whole world was thrown into chaos. In the following weeks, US governors ordered citizens to shelter in place. Universities across the country sent their students home before spring break—for good. Parents had to oversee their younger kids' learning, now exclusively at home. Employees grabbed their laptop and set up an office in their spare bedroom or at the dining room table.

Suddenly, everything became virtual. For our leadership team at Southwestern Consulting, this shift presented an enormous challenge. Like everyone else in the early months of the pandemic, we found ourselves facing circumstances that were completely out of our control. Our business model involved meeting with clients in person, conducting workshops in offices, giving speeches to full rooms, and flying across the country to shadow and support our team members in their home offices. New coaches regularly flew to our corporate offices in Nashville to spend time with the team as well as to receive intensive training.

In addition to one-on-one coaching work, Southwestern Consulting had planned more than ten events in April, May, and June 2020, and members of our leadership team were traveling up to three times a week. In March, however, we experienced an 80 percent cancellation rate in workshops. Clients started calling to put payments on hold. Team members began to question how they could do their jobs.

2020 forced us all to redefine possible—and fast.

As soon as the crisis began, I met with the company's other senior partners. Fortunately, one thing that we knew the pandemic couldn't take from us was our mindset and how we chose to respond to these uncontrollable forces. We were already operating from a positive framework, using the six foundational strategies you are about to learn in this book. As leaders, we also deployed a specific tool called the RAFT™ technique, which we use with coaching clients during difficult times. RAFT works for small challenges, like when a promising client cancels an important

INTRODUCTION: THE POWER OF POSSIBLE

meeting or the family van breaks down right after the warranty expires, as well as for big, life-altering events, like filing for bankruptcy or facing a global pandemic.

At Southwestern Consulting, we found it helpful to apply the RAFT technique during the state of emergency. The technique is simple:

R: Realize an event is happening to you.
A: Accept that the event is occurring.
F: Focus on what you can control.
T: Transform the negative event into positive momentum.

Sounds so easy, right? For our leadership team, using RAFT in March 2020 looked like this: First, we *realized* that the COVID-19 crisis was happening. We didn't try to deny or overdramatize the event; we recognized that the pandemic was wreaking havoc on everyone's lives and businesses. Next, we quickly *accepted* our circumstances. We knew we were facing an unprecedented situation, but we didn't get angry, complain, or waste time pointing fingers. We *focused* on what we could control. By doing that, we eventually *transformed* the negative event into positive momentum, propelling our company and our mission forward. (You'll read more about RAFT in later chapters and in Appendix A of this book.)

As senior partners, we focused on health and safety, but we balanced our actions by making sure not to overreact. We reminded our team members that even though the circumstances seemed unpredictable, there were some things we could control, including our own attitudes and schedules. We encouraged everyone to take ownership of the situation, recognizing that we were all working from home, in a pandemic, and the results would be up to us. We also believed in our mission and had faith that we would succeed.

As a company, we came up with a game plan, arranging video calls, ramping up our communication, keeping our team's health and safety front of mind, and ultimately focusing on our mission of impact. Most significantly, we pivoted all of our workshops to an online model, which was a huge success. By the end of April 2020, our coaches had booked more workshops than they had in April 2019.

Like many people, our leadership team had grand plans for what we were going to accomplish in 2020. Despite COVID-19 throwing a wrench in our lives, we utilized the RAFT technique to help center ourselves in the chaos, working to redefine possible—both individually and as a business.

These techniques have stood the test of time for our business. Now, in this post-COVID world, Southwestern Consulting is getting closer and closer to achieving our mission . . . all thanks to the tools in this book.

LET'S GET STARTED

How did I get here? I certainly don't have it all figured out. But ask anyone who has known me for a long time, and they will agree that I am not the same person I was five or ten years ago.

I, Ron Alford, am writing this book because I believe I was

INTRODUCTION: THE POWER OF POSSIBLE

put on this earth to learn and share. I believe I've been given more than I deserve, and I am truly grateful for God's goodness and grace in my life. I appreciate both the mountaintops and the valleys in my journey. I have hit rock bottom and crawled my way back out of the pit of despair—more than once.

My career is intimately tied to Southwestern Family of Companies, a diverse group of organizations (including Southwestern Consulting) that spans the world and encompasses a range of industries, including leadership training and consulting, sales and leadership coaching, publishing, executive search services, direct sales, real estate, insurance, and travel. Since 1855, Southwestern Family of Companies has been committed to building purpose-driven people, and today, those people are building principle-guided businesses that impact the world.

The principles I'm about to share with you in this book are rooted in the mission and the proven strategies developed by Southwestern Family of Companies, where I have worked since 2003. Many of these techniques and strategies come from decades of receiving successful training within Southwestern's various organizations.

I wrote the first edition of this book in the middle of the global pandemic in 2020–2021. Since then, I've worked hard to hone and expand upon these time-honored concepts by speaking with others and applying the concepts diligently to my own professional and personal life. While the basic content and constructs of this book are the same, this updated and revised edition reflects a broader perspective on the strategies and includes additional stories to provide clarity and deeper meaning. These strategies have continued to make an incredible impact—not only in my own life but also in the lives of the countless people I help and coach.

Before I get started, though, I'd like to officially introduce myself.

I am a senior partner at Southwestern Consulting and the vice president of recruiting at Southwestern Coaching, the sales and leadership, one-on-one coaching arm of Southwestern Consulting. Outside the office, I am an avid endurance runner, having completed many ultrarunning adventures such as the Oregon Cascades 100, a one-hundred-mile trail running race; the Grand Canyon forty-seven-mile Rim-to-Rim-to-Rim run; and the ninety-six-mile trail run around Mount Rainier. Most important, I'm a loving husband and father.

I have learned a tremendous amount about human behavior, mindset, and results by personally coaching hundreds of top executives, leaders, and salespeople from numerous companies in nearly every industry. This work has been a blessing for me. Without a doubt, I know I was put on this earth to help people. But don't think for a moment that I haven't experienced failure, disappointment, and discouragement along the way.

A ROCK-BOTTOM MOMENT

Picture this: A forty-year-old man lies alone on the floor of a cramped apartment, sobbing. The place is not a home or a refuge. It's a makeshift penalty box where the man has been sent to pay for his failures and face his shame. Or so he believes.

INTRODUCTION: THE POWER OF POSSIBLE

It is the summer of 2013—and that man is me.

Until that season I thought I knew who I was: a purpose-minded businessman who could take pride in helping to build a stellar company spanning much of North America; a dedicated family man with a beautiful wife and four-year-old twin boys who were everything to me; and most of all, a man committed to God, who believed he was put on this earth for a clear purpose. Not far away, near Seattle, my dream house was under construction, almost ready to contain the future that I had worked so long and hard to achieve. Professionally, I was someone who helped others succeed and reach their dreams. How was it possible that my own dreams were now in shreds around me on the floor?

I'd like to say my situation was something that made me unique or special, but I can't. Like millions of other people, I was experiencing an unexpected divorce that had turned my entire world upside down. I wasn't accustomed to failure, and my ridiculous ego was worried about what people would think of me—especially my kids. To top it off, money was tight: my production at work had dramatically fallen off since I had been focused on saving my marriage. Everything I had ever built, and everything upon which I had pinned my hopes, seemed utterly meaningless.

As I lay on that apartment floor in despair, though, I suddenly saw myself in a new light. I recognized that I had two identities competing with each other. The first—the tear-stained victim—currently had the upper hand. The victim inside me felt like the world was going to end (and secretly wanted it to). But there was another identity struggling to take hold: the conqueror.

That evening, I finally realized that I had the power to choose which path I would take. I could use my suffering as fuel to create lasting change. I could be a conqueror.

In that apartment, I used the RAFT technique. I realized I could stop whining and wallowing and accept the potential for growth in the pain. The truth is, my divorce had happened, and I could choose how I let the experience define me. I could stop trying to figure out whose "fault" it was that our marriage had ended and start taking responsibility for my role in the situation. Instead of just living in pain, I could move forward by focusing on the things in my control, like my attitude and my actions.

In just a moment, I transformed my life and redefined possible.

This powerful shift gave me perspective. I understood that while my circumstances were tough, they were not the end of the world. Eventually, the kids would be okay. Eventually, I would be okay. (In fact, we would all be so much better than okay!)

In the following weeks, I asked my ex-wife to forgive anything I had done to hurt her so we could pave the way for a good coparenting relationship. I became more involved in church and surrounded myself with people of faith. I took up extreme trail running and set ambitious goals like completing the grueling Grand Canyon Rim-to-Rim-to-Rim run. I poured new energy and vision into my professional life, and soon I was on my way to breaking the Southwestern Coaching sales record.

Today, I am happily remarried to an incredible woman, Desireé, and I have welcomed a beautiful daughter, Hartley, into my life. My boys, Paxton (we call him P. K.) and Van, are more precious to me than ever. I have earned a new, hard-won confidence in who I really am and what I'm capable of doing.

And all this happened because one night in 2013, I decided my pain would be fuel, not poison.

A "NEW YOU" STATE OF MIND

Before I introduce the six strategies, I want to talk about something foundational: mindset.

You must have the right mindset before you can tackle the techniques in this book. Mindset is thought control—mental fortitude. Setting a positive mindset sounds easy, but it is not. It is a lifelong pursuit that allows you to tap into something hidden deep inside you. It makes you acutely aware of your feelings so you can adjust those emotions to be at peak performance. It helps you to eliminate toxic thoughts that hold you back and to unlock your own untapped potential.

With the right mindset, we can elevate our thoughts and temporarily disengage from the stresses of daily life, like doctors' appointments, sales quotas, and travel schedules. With the right mindset, we can face major setbacks and pick ourselves up from that apartment floor. With the wrong mindset, we feel defeated no matter what is going on around us. Anxiety and doubts set in, comparison runs rampant, stress rises, and willpower decreases.

When we focus on mindset, though, we become supercharged, confident we can attain our goals. We feel peaceful, like we've hit the reset button. We connect more deeply with our loved ones. We get excited about the potential around us. We have a raw energy for what is next . . . what is possible.

Creating a positive mindset is so important that I devote time to it daily. For instance, I spend twenty to thirty minutes dreaming, wide awake, when I fly for work or trail run. I pull up a specific playlist that inspires me, and I pray and think about my goals and vision.

As I listen to music, I reflect on who I want to be:

- An extraordinary dad and husband who inspires my wife and three kids by fully using my gifts and talents
- A visionary businessperson and leader—someone who *shows* my team what can happen rather than just hypothesizing about it
- A spiritual person who lives abundantly as a child of God, tapping into the deepest reservoirs of my soul by connecting with my Heavenly Father

Being on a plane or in the woods gives me the space and time to dream freely, without interruptions. Think about where you can go to elevate your thoughts and reset your mind. Some people I know like to drive with the windows down. Others go to their favorite coffee shop. Still others hit a familiar hiking trail or designate a certain room in the house to journal.

Having the right mindset makes it possible for you to identify your purpose and vision. In fact, it's the foundation for every strategy in this book.

INTRODUCTION: THE POWER OF POSSIBLE

IF I CAN REDEFINE POSSIBLE, SO CAN YOU

Helping people tap into their potential has become the highest calling of my life.

I do it because I am a regular guy who doesn't deserve anything but who has experienced the extraordinary power of redefining possible. I truly believe that if I can redefine what possible looks like in my own life, you can too!

The goal of this book is to give you the keys to a new future using proven strategies that will open possibilities that you've yet to imagine. I've already mentioned the RAFT technique that I use when facing challenges or setbacks. In the following chapters, I'm going to explore some foundational strategies that my team and I apply and coach clients on every single day. These strategies are based on six key concepts: focus, ownership, vision, belief, confidence, and faith. These ideas build on themselves in different ways to create a larger picture of what it means to redefine possible. Together, they create the basis for a productive, balanced, and fulfilling life.

Starting from focus and ending with faith, these six essential strategies can literally change your life:

- *Focus:* Focus creates power. Without focus, you will succumb to distractions, and your work will be much less effective. Being intentionally focused will help you get better results in less time.
- *Ownership:* When you take ownership of your life, you hold yourself to the highest possible standard. Taking responsibility for your actions will give you control and help lay the

best possible foundation for future achievements.
- *Vision:* When you combine focus and ownership, you get vision. Vision is the fuel for your life. By casting a compelling vision, you will create energy, excitement, endurance, and empowerment.
- *Belief:* As others have said, your limits begin where your beliefs end. Your beliefs and convictions will help you break through barriers and self-imposed limits and find your calling.
- *Confidence:* When you have unconditional confidence, you will know that you are enough. You will find peace in the face of adversity and learn to embrace your purpose.
- *Faith:* Belief and confidence result in faith. Faith helps you center yourself and identify your core beliefs to add conviction to your work and your life.

When you follow these six strategies that I have outlined, you will naturally create a life of impact! Impact is crucial. I believe it is the reason we've been put on this earth. I have a strong faith in God, and I believe that He cares more about my impact than my accolades. If you want to redefine possible, your barometer cannot be the size of your house, how impressive your job title is, or how many trophies are on your shelf. Instead, it should be how many lives you can positively impact.

INTRODUCTION: THE POWER OF POSSIBLE

YOUR FORMULA FOR LIFE

Now that you have committed to working on your mindset each day—a mindset that is peaceful, positive, dedicated, and focused—you have arrived at the starting line. From there, you can progress through the strategies toward a new way of life. You're going to have to work hard, but with the ideas in this book, you can power through. When you see obstacles looming, take heart. The reward and impact will come when you stay committed to the plan.

The key strategies I will explore in the pages ahead are elements in a formula that will change your life forever. Here's how the formula works:

> Focus + Ownership = **Vision**
> Belief + Confidence = **Faith**
>
> **Vision + Faith + Impact = Redefining Possible**

As I mentioned, I'm far from perfect, but these techniques have transformed my relationships with my family, friends, clients, and coworkers. For example, since I have redefined possible, I don't switch to autopilot anymore when I finish work or return from a business trip. I want to focus on building memories and deep connections with my family. One of the ways Desireé and I do this is to give experiences to our kids on birthdays and holidays instead of big-ticket material items. The kids love going on unforgettable adventures with us—touring Seattle from a helicopter, backpacking in the Cascade mountains, and finding great cabins in small mountain towns—more than any gadget we could give them.

Desireé and I also work to spend individual time with each member of the family. I bring my daughter, Hartley, to various cities she wants to visit, and I take my sons, Van and P. K., on a yearly boys' trip to see our favorite sports teams or to go white water rafting in the Pacific Northwest mountains. Desireé and I work on our marriage by having a "State of the Union" every Sunday night, where we check in with each other for the upcoming week, and recently, we attended a three-day marriage retreat—something we have committed to doing each year. We didn't have big things to fix in our relationship; we just wanted to be proactive so we could be better for each other.

Building healthy relationships, both at home and at the office, is a natural outgrowth of redefining possible. There is work involved, but the results are worth it! As you read this book, remain on the path and avoid mental traps, like excuses, which will tempt you to put this book down and tell yourself you'll read it later. Be guided by determination and an eagerness to learn and grow. Stay open to change. When the lessons come, absorb them and take action. After all, I'm talking about redefining possible for your life—and you only get one life to live, so now is the best time to start.

I hope I've convinced you to keep reading this book. Study these strategies and techniques; let them sink in. You might have to challenge a lot of the things you think are true, but getting "unstuck" is well worth the effort. After all, two of the most insidious words in our vocabularies are *tomorrow* and *someday*.

INTRODUCTION: THE POWER OF POSSIBLE

There's a reason I've identified six key strategies around these core concepts.

They work.

After all, without *vision*, you don't have direction. You just let things happen to you instead of being proactive. You're not on time, and you're not on top of details. You don't follow through on your commitments. You lack focus. You are scattered, stressed, and overwhelmed.

When you don't have *faith*, you feel overwhelmed and hopeless. You live in fear, always scared that something bad is just around the corner. Life without faith is full of shame, guilt, and worry.

But when you have stronger versions of *focus, ownership, vision, belief, confidence,* and *faith,* you will automatically live a life of *impact.* Impact should be your goal. A life without impact is shallow: you become so consumed by your image and self-serving goals, you don't see that people are hurting and in need. You are in your own world—and that's a lonely place to be.

If you see yourself lacking in some of these areas, you may be concerned. But if you take only one thing from reading this book, please let it be this: *it doesn't have to be like that.*

If you are ready for them, the ideas in this book can transform your life. These are proven strategies and time-tested principles. Think of this book as a practical guide on how to implement and live out these established ideas.

You've already taken the first step. Simply by starting this book, you have begun the journey to a new and better you.

This is your season and now is your time to redefine possible.

[STRATEGY ONE]

Sharpen Your Focus

> *"Most people have no idea of the giant capacity we can immediately command when we focus all of our resources on mastering a single area of our lives."*
> —Tony Robbins, best-selling author and speaker

Imagine this: It's 5:30 in the morning when your alarm goes off. "It's Monday," you think. "Time to take on the week!" You've trained yourself to be an early riser, so you turn off the alarm right away, ready to take on the plan you've created for the day. You pour yourself a cup of coffee and start the morning with fifteen minutes of meditation or prayer. After a healthy breakfast, you hit the gym and crush it.

Once at the office, you stick to a thoughtfully planned schedule that includes time for appointments, calls, brainstorming, and more. You are prepared for challenges, so when they come you tackle them with confidence. You're intentional. You're present. You're winning.

You feel joy. You feel alive.

Best of all, you have immense belief in what you are doing. You are productive all day, and people are drawn to you because of the positive attitude you exude. If you're recruiting, you find good people who want to be on your team. If you are selling something, you pitch your product or service with confidence because you know people want to do business with you. If you're giving a presentation, you do it with energy and positivity.

On the way home, you listen to a helpful podcast or audiobook. Then, before you walk in the door, you hit a mental "refresh" to be fully present and available. With your phone tucked away, you devote yourself to your partner or family. You sit down for dinner together. You listen intently as your family members tell you about their day, and you enjoy that quality time. Your schedule might even include having a sitter booked and reservations made for a date night.

Just before bed, you meditate or pray for a few minutes. You express your gratitude for all the little things that went right that day. You never take for granted the gift of life and the opportunity you have to help people every day through your work. When your head hits the pillow, you know you left it all on the field that day, so you sleep soundly.

Sure, you have some tough responsibilities, but you handle them with a light heart, a sense of joy, and enthusiasm. You're open to new goals, new dreams, new levels of achievement. Your relationships are rich and marked by genuine humility; your work life is satisfying and rewarded by prosperity and opportunity. You are

STRATEGY ONE: SHARPEN YOUR FOCUS

known for your authenticity, never worrying about being someone you're not. You have mastery over your attitude, your activities, and your time. You let go of everything you cannot control. You are able to move beyond your mistakes.

On a deep level, you have a strong sense of purpose. You're increasingly dialed into the life you are meant to live. You feel fulfilled. You are driven by your own purpose rather than the agendas of those around you. Everything you desire in life now seems achievable because you have completely redefined what's possible.

Does this seem out of reach?

Many of the people I meet say that they are struggling to achieve the kind of purpose I've just described. They often have a good job, loving relationships, and a nice house. In fact, they may have all the material items they could want, but they're no longer excited about the things they've worked so hard to obtain. Their dream job has become simply a means of paying the mortgage—just one more thing at the top of a long list of responsibilities.

If you're feeling tired, defeated by your circumstances, or unfulfilled in your work, you might have trouble believing that a different type of life is attainable. Fortunately, it's possible. There are strategies you can choose to employ that will unlock the kind of life I just described.

The first strategy I want you to embrace is to sharpen one of the most powerful tools in your possession. I want you to wield it every day.

It's your focus.

WHEN CRISIS HITS

I learned how to maximize my focus during the most challenging trial of my life.

In the summer of 2016, my life was finally back on track. Three years had passed since that heart-wrenching night of despair, feeling crushed by my divorce. I had found love again, and I was preparing to propose marriage to the new love of my life, Desireé. We were excited about blending our two families—her daughter, Hartley, and my twin sons, Van and P. K. Professionally, I had regained my lost momentum and was building a thriving business. I felt stronger than ever.

That all came to a crashing halt with one phone call.

In August that year, my son Van—seven years old at the time—developed what we thought at first might be an allergic reaction to shellfish. His face began to swell and kept getting bigger and bigger. When initial treatments proved ineffective, Van's mom took him to Seattle Children's Hospital for a more comprehensive evaluation. After a round of tests, doctors gave us horrifying news—three words that turned our world upside down.

"Van has leukemia."

I assure you that it is possible for time to stand still and for the earth to stop spinning. Suddenly, nothing else mattered as much as rallying to comfort and protect this little boy whom we all loved so much. We were thrown instantly into the overwhelming task of understanding this strange disease and coming to grips with what the diagnosis meant—for Van, certainly, but for the rest of us as well. What were his chances of survival? What treatments were recommended, and how would they affect him? How would our lives change as we rushed to provide Van with every possible advantage in the battle he now faced?

In November that year, Desireé and I got married in a small, surprise Thanksgiving ceremony. Van was there: thankfully, he was between treatments, so his immune system was strong enough to handle being around others. But the rest of the time was a blur of coping with part-time hospital living, making decisions about treatment options, and watching our boy suffer. On top of that, we had other children who needed our care and comfort, particularly Van's twin, Paxton, who had barely spent an hour apart from his brother in his whole life. In addition to the family stress, I needed to press on at work, which stretched my ability to focus beyond what I thought was possible.

It soon became clear to me what I had to do to survive this crisis. In the following months and years, I would need to truly embody what it meant to redefine possible in the face of hardship. I decided to follow the RAFT technique described in the introduction. First, I realized that one of my worst nightmares was happening—one of our children had cancer. Then I accepted that the event was taking place. I didn't go into a state of denial, pretending that everything was okay, or dive into distractions like numbing out to TV or drinking too much alcohol. I wanted to be the greatest example I could be of strength and *focus* for my kids. By focusing on the most important things—hour by hour, day by day—I was able to transform the crisis from something that threatened to overwhelm and defeat me into an event that solidified my relationships with my family and gave me perspective about what was most important.

Here's what extreme focus looked like for me: When I was at the hospital with Van, I would pretend the rest of the world didn't exist. He had my full attention. When Van was napping, with nurses, or with other family, I would compartmentalize my pain and call my coaches and clients to support them. At home with the rest of the family, I'd think of nothing but being the best possible husband and father. The same was true with my career. I fiercely guarded work time against draining worries and distractions. I also kept a serious focus on my own mental and physical health, remaining committed to my personal fitness and sanity, making each workout count more than ever because I had no time to waste.

No one is ever ready to have a crisis like this, but when such a crisis does appear, it often comes bearing gifts along with challenges. That has certainly been true of this phase in my life. It has made me far more focused and intentional about my relationships, my faith, and my work. I have a much clearer view of what really matters in life and how to set appropriate boundaries and priorities.

Today, my family is healthy and thriving—and so is Van. In November 2019, three and a half years after he was diagnosed, Van was declared cancer-free and got to ring the bell at Seattle Children's Hospital, where he had been treated. We still have plenty of challenges and dysfunction like any family, but our perspective has taken a 180-degree turn. Now, the little victories are more meaningful, and the little failures don't matter quite as much.

STRATEGY ONE: SHARPEN YOUR FOCUS

My experience with managing the difficult early stage of Van's illness showed me a new, unexpected, and deeper meaning of the word *focus*.

THE POWER OF UNRELENTING FOCUS

When I decided to write a book about how to redefine possible, I purposefully started with the concept of focus. I define focus as the state of being intentional and proactive—giving 100 percent of everything I've got. It's a big challenge for most of us, and yet it is the only reason that anyone accomplishes anything of significance. Without focus, I would be, as the saying goes, a "jack-of-all-trades, but a master of none."

I see examples everywhere of what it means to lack focus. People want to get rich quick and lose weight fast; they want to keep up with their neighbors. Then they get bored with what they are doing as soon as they get good at it and decide to try something new.

I've had some very successful clients, and I've found there is a critical quality that sets them apart from the other people I coach. What is it? My most successful clients are the ones who have learned to focus on long-term goals and concentrate over extended periods of time, regardless of what is happening at home or in the global market. This enables them to turn their long-term vision into reality.

Having sustained focus isn't easy. The world lacks focus. We live in a world of distractions, with most of us constantly accessing social media, emails, texts, and the twenty-four-hour news cycle on our watches and phones. During Southwestern Coaching workshops, I often ask my audience, "What's your greatest strength?" Sadly, I've never—not once!—had someone answer, "I am incredible at focusing."

As I mentioned, trail running helps me attain the right mindset. But running also gives me sustained focus. It cuts through all the distractions, stresses, and to-do items that can fill my mind. When I'm deep in the woods of Washington State, where I live, with no people or cars and only a dirt trail ahead of me, I get that beautiful runner's high. I am completely focused on my environment, which helps me to experience the joy of the journey.

This holds true for every experience or task. When I focus, everything becomes richer and more meaningful. I try to maintain focus in everything I do, whether I'm kissing my wife, catching a football pass from my son, making a prospecting call, participating in my fifth Zoom call of the day, or attending church with my family.

Most people go their whole life without learning how to give something 100 percent of their focus. And that's crazy. Without focus, we get scattered, and everything becomes watered down—a lesser version of what it could have been because we've done several things passably well instead of one thing with excellence. We get scared, we hold back, and we are often left wondering what would have happened if we had gone all in.

With focus, however, we become more intentional, which means that we get more done in less time. And with that extra time and laser-sharp focus, we can be unstoppable. As I mentioned,

STRATEGY ONE: SHARPEN YOUR FOCUS

focus is one of the things that helped us reorient ourselves as a company in the early months of 2020 after the outbreak and the global state of emergency. When our leadership team utilized this strategy—along with the other steps in the RAFT technique—we were able to increase our activity levels from the previous year.

If you said, "I'm going to become a master at focusing," it would change your entire life. Because when you focus, you create power for yourself. It's like taking a magnifying glass and harnessing the power of the sun to create fire.

Humans are incredibly capable. Recent studies have shown that the human brain—which has around one hundred billion neurons and a quadrillion synapses that wire the neurons together—is even more powerful than scientists once thought.[1] But with all the technology and activities and choices that are available to us, we often become distracted, and most of us don't live up to our potential. If we could tap into the power of our mind and learn to truly focus, there's no limit to what we could do. We could change the world.

FOUR TECHNIQUES TO SHARPEN YOUR FOCUS

When I coach leaders and executives, I walk them through four steps they can take that will strengthen their ability to focus as never before.

In fact, if you sharpen your focus starting today, within a week you'll see a noticeable difference in your productivity. Here's how to begin putting these four techniques into practice:

1. Eliminate Mental Clutter.

It's essential to recognize a primary enemy of focus: mental clutter. In fact, I cannot overstate the roadblocks that are created when you allow clutter to accumulate in your mind. This kind of clutter comes in many forms:

- *Too much incoming information.* This can be from news alerts, social media, television, podcasts and playlists, emails, texts, and any number of other things.
- *An overcrowded calendar.* This fills your brain (and hours) with more obligations than you can possibly keep up with, which takes your attention away from your income-producing activities.
- *Unresolved conflicts and issues.* These challenges will weigh on you and erode your peace of mind.
- *The daily drumbeat of distractions.* These can include work emergencies (or nonemergencies), demands from family, phone calls out of the blue, text alerts, and last-minute meetings.

The fact is, our culture and lifestyle seem intent on consuming every last kilowatt of our brainpower. All these things can divert our focus from our highest priorities and our primary calling in life.[2]

Studies by Lynn Hasher at the University of Toronto found that mental clutter can lead to cognitive decline in older adults. Excess information can prevent them from processing things that are important,[3] both in the short term (like the time of a

STRATEGY ONE: SHARPEN YOUR FOCUS

dentist appointment) and the long term (like the names of long-time friends). Another study found that even physical clutter in the home and workplace can impact mental health, creating low self-esteem, unhealthy eating habits, and unhappiness,[4] especially among women.

Here's the good news, though: When you are intentional about cutting down the clutter, you will not only feel calmer, but you will also rebound from setbacks more quickly. You will have a sharp focus so you can think more creatively. You will also be more pleasant to be around.

To clear the clutter from your mind, I recommend writing down your to-do list, schedule, and other items you worry about forgetting. In general, you won't be able to hold conversations or even sleep as well when you have thoughts that are weighing on you. When you write these things down, you will see how much easier it is to concentrate. Odds are, you will resist this idea because it is a pain at first. Because it is not yet a habit, it will be uncomfortable. But this is a key step.

In addition to writing down your to-do list and schedule, I recommend keeping a journal for all your random thoughts and setting limits with your electronic devices. I'm not saying you should completely cut out social media, the news, TV, or any other methods that you use to keep in touch with the world—but I do encourage you to limit the amount of information you consume and not to let what you see on those platforms clutter your mind.

2. Choose Your Targets.

Next, to bring more focus into your life, write down your specific goals and plans. Don't be vague.

As a professional sales and leadership coach, I have asked thousands of high-performing executives to send me a copy of their goals. It is shocking to me how many people know conceptually that they should have their goals in writing and yet have not done so. I can't emphasize enough how important this is. I've found that very few of my clients who don't put their goals on paper have viable plans for how to achieve those unwritten goals.

Once you've written out your goals, you'll want to bring them into focus. The first step to doing that is to decide what you really want out of this one life you've been given.

What do you want in your personal life? What do you want in your business/professional life? What do you want in your spiritual life? After you've asked yourself these questions, stop reading this book and take fifteen minutes to write down what you want.

Then, the next question you should ask is, "Do I want it so badly that I am willing to focus on it?" When your answer is yes, then the magic happens. Now you can start to transfer your goals from a piece of paper to your calendar, giving yourself action items and deadlines.

For example, if your goal is to lose weight, you know that you need to eat better or work out more often. By putting your workout times in your schedule, you will be more consistent about showing up at the gym. And having a written workout plan will prevent you from wandering around the gym aimlessly—or worse, giving

STRATEGY ONE: SHARPEN YOUR FOCUS

yourself an excuse not to make it there at all. Instead, you'll know the exercises you need to do when you're there, and because you are focused, you'll be able to finish the same workout that used to take you an hour in thirty minutes. Similarly, by having a specific meal plan to follow, you will meet all your nutritional needs and won't find yourself absentmindedly eating snacks. Grocery shopping for the week will also save you time and money.

What empowers you to make that kind of shift? Focus.

Picture an ideal week in your life, define the related tasks, and then pencil them into your calendar. This can be done on paper or with an Excel spreadsheet or calendar app. For now, be sure to include everything you need or want to do for work, for yourself, and with your family.

It's crucial to be specific. Taking shortcuts or being vague will drastically limit your results. When you start writing down your schedule, set hard start and stop times for time-consuming activities, such as checking email. You'll soon find that you get more done when you know there is an end in sight. Beware of mental traps, such as telling yourself, "Yeah, I'll do it over the next few hours while I finish other stuff." Being intentional about your schedule and blocking out time for specific tasks will make it much easier for you to focus on what is most important. You will also accomplish more throughout the day instead of leaving lots of tasks halfway done.

When you're planning your week, beware of a second trap that we can all fall into: the horrible disease I sometimes call "terminal uniqueness." When you are suffering from terminal uniqueness, you let yourself believe you are so different that your situation allows you to be an exception. You give yourself an out. The reality is that you are usually not that different. Everyone can find a reason to be lazy or avoid applying these tried-and-true principles. Force yourself to follow through and make it happen.

Once you start scheduling the action items that will help you reach your goals, you'll discover that every minute matters more and the minutes you invest will bear more fruit.

3. Guard Your Momentum and Follow Through.

After you have transferred your plans on paper to specific action items in your calendar, the next step is to stay accountable. Find ways to stay committed to the plan so you can continue to gain momentum.

You can start by protecting your schedule. This is especially important when you're working from home. Keep each task or appointment sacred, as if you were a Rottweiler guarding a bone. Do everything you can to prevent that task or commitment from being infringed upon by unplanned interruptions. If you find that your excuse for why you cannot get things done is because other people are "interrupting your day," then you need to be the one to make changes. Psychologists and best-selling authors Drs. Henry Cloud and John Townsend explain that we are always conditioning other people and setting boundaries for how they act and communicate with us.[5] When something is important to you, you will create limits in your schedule, getting whatever needs to be done in the time you allot for it. So if your goal is to leave the office

STRATEGY ONE: SHARPEN YOUR FOCUS

or shut down your computer at home by 5:30 every day so that you can eat dinner with your family, then you need to guard that time. Start work early. Make sure your meetings are efficient. Minimize interruptions. And then at 5:00, begin planning what you need to do the next day so you can finish on time.

Continue to exercise your follow-through muscles, which are just like other muscles: they grow when pushed. Your ability to carry out tasks consistently will improve as much as you let yourself believe it will. As you stay motivated and keep yourself accountable, you will surprise yourself and get better at staying on task.

4. Speak Your New Reality.

Use affirmations to harness your self-talk. When you say empowering statements out loud, you will rewire your brain to believe that focus can and will be one of your greatest strengths.

Study the stories of many great and elite performers—whether they are world-renowned surgeons, historic artists, company founders, or Olympic athletes—and you will likely discover that they practice positive affirmations that lead to thoughts that create excellent results. Our thoughts direct our life,[6] so it's essential to have a list of healthy affirmations you can recite. These statements will adjust your thoughts so that they serve you rather than hold you back.

If you have struggled with using affirmations in the past, don't worry. I will provide ideas to make them work for you. I believe affirmations are so important, in fact, that I have concluded each chapter with targeted lists of what I'm calling "power statements" to give you a head start. (There are also lines for you to write out your own affirmations.) You can learn to make affirmations feel authentic and meaningful. Of course, it takes sustained effort. Practice saying these statements out loud. Modify the phrases until they feel natural to you. Once you've mastered a few affirmations, add some new ones.

Learning to say affirmations to yourself consistently is a foundational habit. If it is awkward or you struggle at first, don't give up. This is a pursuit worth working on forever.

STRATEGY ONE: SHARPEN YOUR FOCUS

POWER STATEMENTS

As you learn to focus, try practicing the following affirmations:

"Focus gives me power."

"I was created to focus on helping other people."

"I am calm and focused in all that I do."

"I choose to focus on the things I can control."

"I'm locked in. Nothing can derail me from reaching my goal."

"My time is precious; I make the most of every opportunity."

"I'm present with every person I talk to."

"I spend my time and energy on meaningful things."

"I let go of any unnecessary worries or habits that distract me from my goals."

SPOTLIGHT ON STRATEGY ONE:
TYLER HJELSETH SHARPENS HIS FOCUS

Imagine that becoming your best self and meeting your specific goals is like taking a cross-country road trip. You map out a route, tune up the engine, and fill up the tank. Then you put the car in gear and hit the gas.

As soon as you leave the driveway, though, a big juicy bug splatters across the windshield, followed by another and another. Before long, your focus has shifted from the road to the smeared mess in front of you. Even if you manage to reach your destination, chances are you'll be stressed and exhausted.

Now you have a picture of what happens when you let daily distractions (bugs) divert you from your plans. Fortunately, it's never too late to pull over, clean up, and get back on the road, this time avoiding the bugs entirely.

Tyler Hjelseth's story is a great example of just how beneficial it can be to refine your focus.

When I began coaching Tyler in 2015, he was a moderately successful financial advisor with Northwestern Mutual Wealth Management Company. His production numbers were better than average but nothing that would get him noticed beyond his home

STRATEGY ONE: SHARPEN YOUR FOCUS

market of Tacoma, Washington. He wanted much more than that but was short on ideas as to how to get there.

One of the first things I advised him to do was keep a time awareness log. The goal was not to become a slave to the clock. Rather, it was to use the log to make every minute count. Tracking every block of time during his day was a hassle, but Tyler had a strong vision and purpose, and he was dedicated to doing it.

It didn't take long to realize that one of Tyler's biggest disadvantages was self-imposed: he often let distractions and a relaxed approach to his schedule rob him of precious minutes. By keeping a log, he was able to see what it cost to schedule time for making prospecting calls and then let it slip away by answering a nonurgent email, updating his fantasy football lineup, or stopping by a colleague's office "just for a second." Those choices not only cost him time but also stalled his momentum, resulting in lost opportunities.

Tyler quickly learned to see the value in a single minute and to guard each one. "I saw that if I blew ten minutes, I might as well tear up a $20 bill," he admitted.

Next, I helped Tyler see that he also lacked focus in how he selected his clients. By trying to attract anyone and everyone as a client, he would never reach his goals. Setting his sights on a higher-caliber client—and giving his new team members the clients who had a lower net worth—meant changing his mindset and narrowing his focus.

To help him do that, I said, "Brother, if I came into your office right now and handed you $250, what could you do with that? Are you likely to throw it away?" No one would want to toss $250. And yet that's what Tyler was doing every time he spent two hours in a client meeting that had very little potential rather than building up his team to handle the client load and then delegating those opportunities so he could focus on his target market of business owners, executives, and physicians.

As our coaching relationship developed, Tyler became much more careful in screening and solidifying his own potential leads. By the end of his first year of coaching, he had nearly doubled his production totals and led all Northwestern Mutual advisors for new clients in his region. In 2016, his production nearly doubled again, and he was once more named a New Client Leader. Then in May 2018—still not yet thirty years old—Tyler qualified for Northwestern Mutual's Forum Symposium, an elite group of the company's top 2 percent of advisors.

I often saw myself in Tyler while coaching him— not just in a flashback to when I was in my midtwenties and in need of more focus, but also as a businessman,

STRATEGY ONE: SHARPEN YOUR FOCUS

father, and husband today. (Believe me, I still need to work on remaining focused!) It was a reminder that achieving optimum focus is a daily practice none of us ever outgrow.

[STRATEGY TWO]

Own Your Past, Present, and Future

> *"Responsibility equals accountability equals ownership. And a sense of ownership is the most powerful weapon a team or organization can have."*
> —Pat Summitt, legendary basketball coach

Anyone who has been in a leadership role knows to be wary of the things "you don't know that you don't know." It's called having a blind spot. We all have them, and all sorts of unexpected truths can hide there.

Like all people, leaders are prone to habits that can hamper team effectiveness, but they can easily remain unaware of those bad behaviors unless they ask hard questions and open themselves up to tough answers. It's intimidating to ask for feedback. But without that openness, team members rarely have the chance, or feel safe enough, to offer feedback about the boss.

Nearly thirty years ago, when I was a young salesman working for Southwestern Advantage, my manager, Jeff Rogers, taught me how to receive feedback—an experience that altered my life forever. That summer I was leading a team of thirty university students from Seattle—students I had recruited, onboarded, and trained over the years. Despite my high hopes and enthusiasm, nearly one-third of these students didn't finish the summer program. Initially, I put the blame on them, telling myself they were "quitters." But Jeff sat me down and told me that if I wanted to succeed in business, I needed to ask for feedback. He encouraged me to set up a meeting with each student where I would ask three to five questions. Jeff instructed me that I could only listen, and I couldn't defend myself or our company.

I followed his advice . . . and I hated every second of it.

Initially, I was resistant, prideful, and defensive. I thought the meetings were a waste of time. Yet soon I realized that I had overpromised and underdelivered; I hadn't emotionally prepared the students for the way they would feel going door-to-door. Their feedback changed how I approached onboarding, and as time went on, I got much better at retention.

Today, I follow a systemized practice with the coaches on my team at Southwestern Consulting where I solicit anonymous feedback about myself and my management practices. I do this on a regular basis, depending on how long the person has been with me.

At our company, we use a simple survey called the True-You Interview (included in the back of the book).

Here are some of the questions from the True-You Interview:

- What are my strengths? What do you see as my strengths

STRATEGY TWO: OWN YOUR PAST, PRESENT, AND FUTURE

in everyday life and business?
- What are my weaknesses? What doesn't work about the person I am being?
- How can I improve as a leader? What do other people count on me for? What do other people know I can't be counted on for?

When asking for feedback, it's tempting to only take ownership of the positive things. That's easy. But true ownership means honestly facing those things that need improvement or that need to disappear entirely. True ownership means being willing to take responsibility. The pursuit of excellence always involves clearing roadblocks or blind spots, even ones that are highly personal. If we want to grow, we need to hear the truth, even if someone tells us that we said "um" thirty-seven times in a ten-minute presentation or that we're consistently late to calls or meetings.

Feedback is just another way of asking for and receiving help!

Asking for feedback isn't easy, especially at first, but if you ask for it enough, you'll start to see patterns of ways you can improve. You'll also learn how to glean the truth from both good and bad feedback. At each end of the spectrum there are responses that you can safely ignore. This is true for all surveys. Some people will decide they don't like you, no matter what, and take the opportunity to unload a long list of grievances. Others will think you hung the moon and share nothing but glowing praise. But in the vast middle there is often feedback that shows up again and again. Those are the clues you are looking for.

A few years ago, several of my coaching clients mentioned in feedback surveys that I can be too soft and easy on them. These clients wanted me to be tough on them and more direct—they wanted me to hold them accountable for the things they had promised to do, like writing down their goals or delegating certain tasks. After hearing their feedback, I thought, "They're right! That's unacceptable, and I need to focus on this until it's fixed." I took ownership and made the effort to better serve *all* my clients—not just the ones who liked my soft approach—and my clients experienced significant personal and work-related growth.

In addition to soliciting feedback from my clients, I hold feedback sessions with my team. Recently, my assistant, Layla, told me that my tendency to send her tasks at the last minute was creating stress. While I thrive under pressure, Layla does not. For a month, she had tiptoed around the issue, using humor about how I needed to get myself together. I didn't get the hint, so she finally leveled with me when I asked for her feedback: she said that she needed me to send her information several days before something was due. I used the RAFT technique. I realized Layla was upset, accepted ownership of the situation, and focused on making changes. Now Layla is much less stressed (the situation was transformed!).

Fighting your ego and accepting constructive criticism is one of the biggest challenges to taking ownership. But if I can do it, anyone can!

STRATEGY TWO: OWN YOUR PAST, PRESENT, AND FUTURE

THREE TYPES OF FEEDBACK

What comes to mind when you hear the word *feedback*? You might imagine a boss sitting in a closed-door office, talking to a nervous employee at their annual review. In that scenario, the boss would ideally start by giving positive feedback, saying something like, "Mira, your program saved the company $15,000 last year in energy costs!" Then the boss would discuss ways Mira could improve, like learning the new project management software that the department implemented last month or by meeting other budgeting milestones.

The boss-employee annual review is a good example of *factual feedback*: it's verifiable, measurable, and unemotional. Factual feedback compares someone's performance to measures that were previously set in place and evaluates people in similar roles. It provides neutral feedback and a barometer for how things are going at a certain stage—for example, whether a new hire has met certain standards by the end of their probation period or how far someone needs to go to hit their monthly numbers.

Sports is full of factual feedback. It tells us what the score is at the end of the first quarter or how many rushing yards a running back gained in a game. In 2017, the New England Patriots used factual feedback to win Super Bowl LI. The Atlanta Falcons had built a 28–3 lead midway through the third quarter and had the Patriots' defense on their heels. The Patriots looked at the Falcons' passing statistics, and they realized Matt Ryan, the Falcons' quarterback, had gotten too comfortable running the offense. The Patriots adjusted their defensive strategies to put more pressure on the quarterback and made the biggest comeback in Super Bowl history.

Factual feedback is great, but in the coaching world, we realize many clients don't need more information. They need drive, purpose, and the acknowledgment that they are performing well. *Motivational feedback* appeals to people's emotional side. It gives information that will inspire them to move forward. Motivational feedback can come from coworkers, friends, and family as well as conference speakers and mentors. It can be seen in cheering crowds and encouraging coaches. It celebrates improvement and gets people to hustle and compete by triggering their adrenaline and endorphins.

Motivational feedback can also come from books, videos, or podcasts. I love to read historical biographies of people who have overcome major obstacles or have made a tremendous impact over time. I also listen to a top-ranked business podcast and an inspirational wellness show that brings in forward-thinking guests.

The last type of feedback is *educational feedback*. This happens when an expert provides input to help people meet their goals. This type of feedback can be informative, teaching people something that they didn't know or helping them learn a new skill. It is correctional coaching. Teachers, professors, mentors, field experts, and coaches provide educational feedback by offering tools and information to facilitate growth. With educational feedback, a chef might tell his apprentice, "I love the spices you added to this dish, but next time use a little less garlic so it doesn't overwhelm the other flavors." Or a professor might tell a college student,

STRATEGY TWO: OWN YOUR PAST, PRESENT, AND FUTURE

"You made some great points in your speech, but you need to talk more slowly so that your audience will remember what you said."

As a coach, I try to provide all three types of feedback to my clients. I also seek out factual, motivational, and educational feedback for myself: I look at my numbers, hire coaches and experts, talk with trusted friends and family, and use recommended resources.

By utilizing each one of these three types of feedback, you will learn how to take ownership of your past, present, and future so you can grow.

THE IMPORTANCE OF BEING ACCOUNTABLE

Taking ownership means accepting personal responsibility for your actions—whether the results are negative or positive. It means admitting when you mess up and embracing ownership of the way you spend your day, the choices you make, and your plans for the future. It means letting people know that you are going to follow through, execute your plans, and be accountable to yourself and to others.

Taking ownership isn't always easy. But not taking ownership comes with its own kind of pain.

When you don't take ownership of your mistakes, you can't take ownership of the good things in life either, such as your positive choices and the plans you've made for your future. And if you don't own your past and your present, how can you have a clear vision of the future?

Not only that, avoiding responsibility for your failures takes a lot of effort. You can easily spend more energy escaping responsibility than embracing important things like your mission, vision, values, and principles. When that happens, you set yourself up to feel like a failure. Shame and guilt can creep in as well as self-pity and self-absorption.

Taking ownership means that you are willing to listen and not get defensive when your partner tells you he or she feels ignored every time you pick up your phone during a meal. It means that you are willing to examine the truth behind the negative feedback you received at work rather than point out what your coworker is also doing wrong. It means that you are willing to grapple with uncomfortable truths about yourself—that maybe you have been self-centered, or too focused on work, or abrupt with your close friend or roommate. It also means you are willing to make changes and ask the people you have hurt for forgiveness.

Taking ownership may sound like a lot of work, but it is freeing. As you become accountable for your own past and present, you naturally stop making excuses and blaming others. You start owning up to your mistakes and fixing them when possible. In fact, when you take ownership, you naturally find yourself doing what you say you are going to do, staying accountable, and making choices out of integrity rather than avoidance. You begin to feel as though you are living up to your calling and your potential, perhaps for the first time ever. And you earn the respect of the people around you, which is rewarding on so many levels.

How do you own your past, present, and future? It's simple: say no to familiar lies and yes to empowering truths.

Let's start with the lies.

FIVE FAMILIAR LIES THAT KEEP YOU STUCK

When people avoid taking ownership, they rationalize their actions. Merriam-Webster defines *rationalization* as "a way of describing, interpreting, or explaining something (such as bad behavior) that makes it seem proper, more attractive, etc."[7]

I like the idea of breaking down the word *rationalize* into "rational" and "lies," because that's what you're doing when you rationalize: you're being dishonest with yourself or with others.

Think about some of the rationalizations you may have heard—or embraced—recently:

1. "Everybody does it."

This is one we've all heard since we were little kids. I hear it all the time with my kids: "My brother/sister did it!" When we say that everyone else does it, we think it justifies what we're doing: If you're always showing up fifteen minutes late to work, then I can come in late too. If you're not totally honest about how much work you did on a group project, then I can fudge my efforts a little bit too. If you're taking more than your fair share, then I will too.

If my coworkers, friends, and neighbors are doing it, then it must be okay.

But having integrity and taking ownership of your actions is not about being comfortable with the way things are or what everyone else is doing. It's about embracing the way things should be. Taking ownership means that your ethics are all that matter. No one else's standards should be important except for your own. If you're constantly comparing yourself to what everyone else does, you'll never successfully take ownership of your life.

Redefining possible is about recognizing that "everybody else does it"—and then choosing to go in the opposite direction.

2. "It's not my job."

This rationalization avoids responsibility *and* passes blame. It might show up when you start finger-pointing at a client, a family member, or one of your team members.

As I said earlier, taking ownership means taking responsibility. It also means going the extra mile without looking for credit—and making this a habit. You may have to do things that are below your pay grade. But the goal here is to exceed the expectations of your coworkers, your boss, your kids, and your partner. You should care so much about them and their expectations that job descriptions and compliments don't matter to you.

You may not be rewarded or noticed in the moment for taking on additional or unwelcome tasks, but the benefits will always come back to you. As Cindy Johnstone, the executive vice president and treasurer of Southwestern Family of Companies, often says: "The people doing the work always get the reward. Sometimes now, often later, but always eventually."

3. "I'm only human."

Average people are willing to take themselves off the hook so quickly. It's easy to do that—we are only human. We're not perfect. (Of course, neither were the people we often hold up as heroes, such as Dr. Martin Luther King Jr., Mother Teresa, and Nelson Mandela.)

STRATEGY TWO: OWN YOUR PAST, PRESENT, AND FUTURE

But redefining possible is not about being average or settling for mediocrity. If you want heightened results, you must think in a heightened way. Just because you're not a superhero doesn't mean you get to bend the rules or give up. When you take ownership, you become accountable for every choice you make. You own your life and your decisions. You listen, plan, take responsibility, and do the right thing. You say, "I'm going to give my best every single day and not make excuses. I know I'm going to mess up because I'm not perfect, but when I do, I'll learn from my mistakes and try not to repeat them."

As humans, we tend to judge ourselves by our best intentions. But in the end, we'll be judged by our worst acts—the areas where we cut corners or the things we discounted because we told ourselves, "It's just human nature."

4. "It's not important."

People use this rationalization when they want to qualify their actions or blow them off. But little things eventually become big things, and if you don't own the little things, you'll be even less likely to own them when they grow to become major problems.

Take lying, for example. Dishonesty can start small, like telling your boss that you were in off-site meetings and appointments for the whole afternoon when you really came home early and took a nap. But if you believe that a few missed hours at work aren't important, you'll be more likely to tell yourself that cheating on your taxes or even on your partner isn't that bad either.

I believe that, as the Bible says, if you are responsible and diligent with the so-called little things, you'll be given more (see Luke 16:10). If you want responsibility, if you want to live a significant life, if you want to live out whatever your definition of success is, you will understand it's the little things that matter most. Or, to take it one step further, once you start taking ownership, you'll see that nothing is really that small. It's *all* important.

5. "But I am/have _____." (Apply label here.)
"But I'm tired," "I don't have enough energy," or "I have ADHD/dyslexia/a bad memory/fill in the blank here." People love labels. They may hear something a parent, friend, or doctor said about them, and suddenly they have adopted a label they can use for the rest of their lives to rationalize why they can't do something.

When people make these excuses, it's because they don't have a strong enough vision, they don't have clarity about their goals, and they lack the dedication to follow through on their commitments. Obviously, we all experience periods of time where we feel anxious or tired or scattered or forgetful. But many of us like to paint a picture of why we're different—and then use it to justify why we can't do something. It's important to take ownership of any shortcomings you may have used as an excuse. Owning that you have ADHD, owning that your energy levels are down because of overwork, or owning that you can't remember small details is a big step toward redefining possible. Once you take ownership of these labels, you'll find that you're able to move past them, overcoming any hindrances they might usually put in your way.

STRATEGY TWO: OWN YOUR PAST, PRESENT, AND FUTURE

In his book *David and Goliath*, Malcolm Gladwell points out that 30 percent of entrepreneurs have some kind of dyslexia. But those entrepreneurs overcame their perceived weaknesses to create highly successful businesses. Interestingly, Gladwell also points out that an equal percentage of people in prison have dyslexia.[8]

It all goes to show that you create your reality.

THE EMPOWERING TRUTH ABOUT YOUR WORDS

Affirmations are a tool you can use to take ownership of your life. Affirmations need to be in the first person, using "I" not "we." They need to be in the present tense, meaning "I am" or "I have."

These phrases should reflect what you are currently doing, not what you are going to do. And they need to include powerful words that convey emotions and create a picture in your mind. For instance, instead of saying, "I'm going to do my best," you might try stating, "I'm an unstoppable force!" These affirmations, or "power statements," will help you take ownership of your life every step of the way.

Affirmations work because, ultimately, words matter. There is a lot of science behind the use of affirmations. For example, a detailed study published in *Social Cognitive and Affective Neuroscience* concludes that affirmations can alter our neural activity and change our behavior.[9] An article in *Psychology Today* also indicates that people who practice affirmations are better at problem-solving.[10]

Practicing affirmations is one way you can do some self-coaching. Affirmations are one of the most effective ways to break through negative thought patterns and rewire your mind. Your thoughts and words alter your behavior and actions, which affect your results—which then, in turn, transform your reality.

Affirmations can be a valuable anchor for you. They are constant, and they make every principle in this book sustainable. As the late motivational speaker Zig Ziglar was known for saying, "People often say that motivation doesn't last. Well, neither does bathing—that's why we recommend it daily."

Be prepared that your mind might fight you in the beginning. Changing your thought patterns will be difficult at first, but your brain is surprisingly adaptable.[11] So make a commitment to redefine possible by pushing outside your limits and breaking through complacency.

You can let the people surrounding you, as well as the news, society, and the world itself, program you to think a certain way. But if you let the outside world dictate your thinking, you'll never take ownership of your own life. The best path? Take control of your thoughts with affirmations.

Once you have your focus honed and your sense of ownership in place, you have a great opportunity to develop a clear and effective vision.

STRATEGY TWO: OWN YOUR PAST, PRESENT, AND FUTURE

POWER STATEMENTS

When you rewire your brain to speak the truth rather than lies, you are essentially recreating what's possible in your life. Here are some affirmations I've found helpful for taking ownership:

"If it's meant to be, it's up to me." (See Robert Schuller's similarly titled book on positive thinking.)

"When I say I'm going to do something, I do it, no matter what."

"My word is my bond."

"I own this day."

"I follow through."

"I can. I will. I'm going to _____."

"Every hour gets my best; every person gets my best."

"I own every part of my life, and I am better because of it."

"I know my strengths and weaknesses, and I use this information to make myself a better person."

_____

_____

_____

_____

_____

_____

_____

_____

_____

SPOTLIGHT ON STRATEGY TWO:
TERRI RICKARD TAKES OWNERSHIP OF HER CAREER

Terri Rickard knows, more than almost anyone, the importance of taking ownership. Her father, an addict, was in and out of prison during most of her childhood—and because she was named after her father and shared his fiery spirit, she often heard that she was "just like him." Terri was determined not to let others' expectations and her family's past dictate her future, though. As a young girl, with the help of her mentors, she took ownership of her life and excelled in school, becoming the first person in her family to graduate from college.

Terri continued that commitment to ownership in her career, creating a successful cross-departmental training program in her first job out of college. Despite her success, she felt led to pursue other opportunities. "So I started praying for direction and researching my options," she said.

Terri began looking for a job in business where she could learn and grow. After a few months, she got connected with Henry Bedford, the chairman and CEO of Southwestern Family of Companies. When she met Henry and learned about Southwestern's mission to build people and help others, she knew she was in the

STRATEGY TWO: OWN YOUR PAST, PRESENT, AND FUTURE

right place. Henry hired her on the spot to be his executive assistant, and he became her business mentor.

Terri was initially hesitant about going into business; she had a history degree and knew little about being an entrepreneur. But what she lacked in business experience, she made up for in dedication and her commitment to taking ownership. Early on, Terri noticed that the family of companies lacked a cohesive travel strategy. Each company was using a different outside travel agency, and multiple employees were booking travel on their own. As a result, Terri recalled, "Southwestern was not tracking its full spend with specific travel suppliers, nor was it utilizing its volume to maximize supplier partnerships and discounts."

Coordinating travel and minimizing expenses weren't part of her daily duties, but Terri was eager to take ownership and find solutions. "For me, taking on other work wasn't a chore or a burden," she explained. "It was an opportunity to support and serve my colleagues, our business, and our mission." Working with the accounting department, she figured out how to streamline the travel process, going through boxes of paperwork and expense reports that were brought in from the warehouse. With Henry's blessing, Terri created an internal travel program for the company's (then) sixteen operating divisions, managing more than $5 million in annual travel spend. Within just a few years of collecting company travel data, conducting intensive industry research, and perfecting the vendor contract negotiation process, she had achieved savings of over $500,000.

In 2016, Terri launched Southwestern Travel Group to help other businesses save money on group travel, focusing on conferences, incentive trips, and school trips. As president, she has worked to make Southwestern Travel Group a trusted travel solutions provider by offering custom travel experiences, complimentary client consultations, and detailed planning, all while maximizing value and convenience.

In early 2020, Southwestern Travel Group was on track to have its best year yet—and then COVID-19 upended the industry. "Suddenly," said Terri, "every booking was canceled or pushed to a future date." She soon realized she would have to take ownership of the situation and adapt. "I was quickly reminded of the RAFT technique, which I learned during my one-on-one coaching program," Terri remembered. "Once I was able to realize the event had happened and then accept my situation, I focused on the things I could control, like my attitude and my schedule. This helped me transform my situation."

First, she worked with her staff to settle all the

STRATEGY TWO: OWN YOUR PAST, PRESENT, AND FUTURE

company's open accounts. Then they began increasing communication, reaching out to potential clients to let them know Southwestern Travel Group would be there when they were ready to resume traveling. The staff also brainstormed new offerings for the company, such as virtual experiences that could be used to enhance the in-person travel experience. "At work, we are encouraged to never walk past a problem," Terri said. "We're continuing to find new ways to rebuild and improve our offerings. We take ownership by getting into the details of our business, and we find unique solutions that will serve our clients—both now and in the future."

[STRATEGY THREE]

Clarify Your Vision

"Create the highest, grandest vision possible for your life, because you become what you believe."
—Oprah Winfrey, global media leader and philanthropist

Nelson Mandela is an incredible example of someone who had vision—and who lived his whole life with that vision as his guiding light. In the mid- to late-twentieth century, South Africa was run by a very small minority group that ruled with an iron fist. Having gained South Africa's independence from Britain, the members of this minority group were like elite monarchs. They practiced apartheid, discriminating against nonwhites, creating unjust laws, and enforcing racial segregation. In response, the South African majority group began to organize strikes, demanding basic rights like being able to buy food and to vote.

Nelson Mandela, who was part of this oppressed majority group, had a vision to create a free South Africa. He launched a campaign of nonviolent protests and proposed nondiscriminatory legislation. His vision was so strong that he was able to maintain it even through decades of imprisonment. From 1963 to 1990, Mandela oversaw the rebellion from his jail cell. He was able to control South Africa's economy and to organize strikes. He challenged racism head-on and forged the path for South Africa to find democracy.

Mandela's vision never wavered. People threw him in prison, tried to bribe him, and even attempted to kill him. But he never compromised. In 1993, he was awarded the Nobel Peace Prize for his work in ending apartheid, and in 1994, Nelson Mandela was inaugurated as the first democratically elected president of South Africa.[12]

THE VALUE OF VISION

We can all agree that Nelson Mandela had extraordinary vision.

But what does that mean? When I say the word *vision*, I'm not talking about eyesight.

Vision is seeing a future that hasn't happened yet. Vision is the light at the end of the tunnel—the image that guides you even when things are dark. Your vision is the picture of what things will look like when you're living on purpose, hitting on all cylinders, and achieving your goals. When you create a powerful picture of the life you desire to lead, you begin to live out that picture as if the elements in it were already true.

With vision, you do everything with more energy, more motivation, and more excitement. I think of vision as a tool—the GPS that directs your path. A well-defined vision eventually becomes

STRATEGY THREE: CLARIFY YOUR VISION

so true to you that it feels like a calling. Vision also gives you clarity and focus.

In contrast, life without vision is completely unplanned. Instead of taking action, you let things happen and then react. Your feelings run the show instead of your rational plans. Without vision, you can't see clearly, so you become distracted from your true goals.

Having a clear vision is crucial if you want to redefine possible.

Vision is particularly useful when making decisions or dealing with difficult situations, because people tend to have one of three reactions to adversity. The first group is paralyzed by it, the second group struggles through it, and the third group adapts to it and becomes stronger. What makes these three groups so different? Their response has everything to do with the strength of their vision.

The first group is made up of people who don't have vision. When they hit a wall, that is all they see. They get stuck, unable to move forward in any way. The second group of people have a goal but lack vision. A goal will only take them so far, though. When adversity hits, they will make an excuse for why they didn't succeed. The third group is comprised of people who have a clear vision. These people are unstoppable. When they run smack into the wall, they barely acknowledge it. Their vision is so crystallized that they immediately look for ways under, over, around, or through the obstacle.

The other day, I was on a conference call with someone in real estate who said that she had been having a rough year because inventory was so low. "I'm so tired," she said. "I've been working so hard; I'm just exhausted."

When I heard that, I wondered what the woman really meant by saying she was tired. Did she need to take a nap so she would feel more rested? Or was she feeling mentally exhausted, discouraged, or burned out? Burnout is common in the workplace, especially with our constant connection to our phones and computers. It can be a real issue if you allow it to be one, and I agree that it's important to recharge, take mental breaks, and listen to your body. Sometimes, however, it takes more than self-care to address burnout, and that's because it's not just the result of simply working long hours.

In my experience, usually when my clients say something along the lines of "I'm so tired," they're not literally tired. What they really mean is they have a vision problem. That is, they don't have the vision needed to propel them through difficult client negotiations, unforeseen circumstances, long days, and other work-related challenges.

Lack of vision can be linked to other underlying issues. For example, if you experience something painful that derails you for an extraordinary length of time, then you might have a vision problem. If you give up quickly, struggle with motivation, are easily distracted, mentally check out, start work late, and cut out early, you might be lacking vision.

Vision is not supposed to be easy, because you're working toward something big—something uncommon and extraordinary. Vision *should* be hard and scary. Your vision must be more

STRATEGY THREE: CLARIFY YOUR VISION

powerful than the strength of your excuses. As the story of Nelson Mandela shows, the strength of your vision is what allows you to overcome hardships. You will move past current obstacles because you can see the payoff—whether it's starting a business or completing a triathlon.

Vision is the answer for why you do anything. A clear vision helps you determine what you want out of life and what steps you must take to reach your goals. With vision, you wake up early if you're a morning person, starting work before everybody else—or if you're a night owl, you work late, finishing after everyone else. With vision, you work smart, think creatively, problem solve, and come up with new ideas. Your vision is so strong that you think about it all the time. It's part of you!

When you create a vision that's crystal clear, it shines a light on your path. It guides you back every time you get off course and helps you see what's possible before anyone else does. It helps you maintain your priorities. With vision, you can redefine what's possible within your mind's eye so you can take action to make it happen in real life. Having an image of what you want to achieve allows you to move faster and become more efficient and effective. Once you get in touch with your vision, you become an unstoppable force.

I often say that vision is like fuel for a fire. A fire will burn hot and last for a long time, but only if you tend to it regularly. Start the process by looking at the things you do on a regular basis. Why are you doing them? If you don't have a compelling reason, then eliminate those activities from your life. Focus on the things that have a specific and clear *why* behind them. Decide that you'll stop going through the motions—and that you'll live a life of vision instead.

In this chapter, I will teach you how to define your vision, write it out, and make sure it's easy to follow. Here are three tools to help you clarify your vision and begin to turn it into a reality.

TOOL #1: YOUR VISION WORKSHEET

Because the concept of having a vision is intangible, I want you to do something to make it concrete. Think of a trait or characteristic you would like to have. Maybe you want to be resilient or perseverant. Perhaps you want to be loving or servant-minded, to think big, or to overcome challenges. Well, that can be part of your vision.

To turn your vision into a more concrete plan, grab a pencil and paper and get ready to ask yourself some questions. You are going to make three lists, which have historically been called the "be-do-haves." The be-do-have approach is something that Stephen Covey, Tony Robbins, and other great motivational speakers have talked about for decades. Here's the model:

Who do you want to be? First, make a list of ten characteristics that detail the person you want to be. Think of it this way: How would you want the people at your funeral to describe you? What characteristics or traits would you want them to mention? This is the essence of what and who you are as a person.

1. _____
2. _____
3. _____

STRATEGY THREE: CLARIFY YOUR VISION

4. _____
5. _____
6. _____
7. _____
8. _____
9. _____
10. _____

What do you want to do? Next, make a list of ten things you want to do. Think about where you want to go, what you want to achieve, or even what awards you want to win. Go crazy with these and think big. This should be *fun!*

1. _____
2. _____
3. _____
4. _____
5. _____
6. _____
7. _____
8. _____
9. _____
10. _____

What do you want to have? Finally, make a list of ten things you want to have. While your "be" and "do" lists are most important, your "have" list will help you clarify your goals. It might include having a bigger house for your growing family, six months of savings for emergencies, or the latest exercise bike for when you can't get to the gym. Let your imagination flow and be specific and vivid.

1. _____
2. _____
3. _____
4. _____
5. _____
6. _____
7. _____
8. _____
9. _____
10. _____

It's important to make these lists in order of "be," "do," and "have." Many people want to jump in with the "haves," but the "haves" are the direct result of the qualities, habits, actions, and intellect you possess—the items on your "be" and "do" lists. First, you need to decide what type of person you want to be, and then you must do the things that kind of person does so you can gain the things you want to have.

Your lists might look like this:

- I want to *be* fit, dedicated, positive, motivated, passionate, determined, disciplined, purpose-driven, intentional, resilient, and selfless. I want to be a loving partner, excellent parent, and reliable friend.
- I want to *do* my weight-training workout four times a

STRATEGY THREE: CLARIFY YOUR VISION

week, wake up at 6:00 every morning, go to my place of worship every weekend, run a marathon, swim with dolphins, hike the Pacific Crest Trail, have date night every week, take two personal development courses, coach my daughter's soccer team, pay for an extended family vacation, and make senior partner at work.

- I want to *have* a larger house with an office where I can more easily work from home, an SUV with room for my son's baseball equipment, a balanced portfolio that can withstand market fluctuations, enough time to pursue my fitness goals, engaged family time, my name on three books, a cabin on the lake where I grew up, well-rounded kids, and a team at work to help me best manage my time.

The things you write on your lists become tied to your actions. For instance, your lists will help you to see why getting out of bed earlier is going to help you reach your endgame. Here's how it works:

With your vision in mind, you wake up at a specific time, rising with purpose and with a plan—you don't just wander into the day. Because you already believe you're a fit person, you have a plan for exactly what to eat, and you enjoy a healthy breakfast. You do some sort of exercise, visualization, or devotional meditation. Your morning routine helps you get your head right before you go conquer the world.

If you have a vision of being a selfless person, then during your day, you focus on service-oriented goals. You ask, "Whom can I serve? How can I bring my product or service or idea to the world or to this person in a way that might impact his or her life?" You don't make the day all about your awards, your plaques, your problems, or your numbers.

The more you focus on your vision, the more you will become your vision. You have to think about your vision before it can actually happen. Having a vision means having a plan: living with intentionality and being focused on what you want one year ahead, five years ahead, ten years ahead, and so on.

TOOL #2: YOUR VISION BOARD

Once you have made your lists, the next step in developing a clear vision for your life is to tie your words to vivid images by creating a vision board.

First, think about your "be-do-haves." Find pictures that represent each item on your list. Then, once you have found those pictures, you can combine them in a way that is meaningful. Your vision board can include anything—such as quotes, words, or pictures—that gets you fired up about working toward your vision.

I want to warn you about a common mistake people can make at this stage. Sometimes people start by looking through magazines to find pictures that catch their eye and then using those pictures for their vision board. The problem is that if you approach the activity this way, you are letting a magazine define your vision, and it will end up being a limited version of what you need or want. Instead, identify the kind of life you desire to lead and then find specific words or pictures to reinforce that vision.

STRATEGY THREE: CLARIFY YOUR VISION

For your vision board to be most effective, you need to make it as detailed as possible, thinking about the people, actions, and emotions that accompany a particular vision or goal.[13] In fact, some psychologists prefer using the term "action boards" to focus on the actions needed to get that particular job, renovate your house, or complete your first marathon.

Once your vision board is completed, use it! Having images of those goals gathered in one place will help you focus on what is important to you. Keep your vision board somewhere you can see it every day so that your vision is literally within sight.

For my own vision board, I found pictures online that matched my vision, printed and cut them out, and glued them on poster board. It was simple, and my vision board continues to be a powerful tool for me. I have it prominently displayed in my office so I can stare at it every day while I'm working toward my goals.

It's not just about hanging a vision board and calling it "done," though. To effectively reach the goals on your vision board, you need to associate those goals with specific actions.[14] So look at your vision board consistently each day, visualizing the steps it will take to reinforce your new habits. By doing this, you will activate the motor cortex of the brain.[15] Your vision board will become a trigger to motivate you into action.

That means you'll work harder, wake up earlier, stay up later, and do all the extra things necessary to achieve your vision. In fact, when your vision is strong enough, detailed enough, and meaningful enough—when it includes not just what you want to have but also who you want to be and what you are willing to do—you'll actually find that your subconscious mind starts working for you.

This exercise will help you perform activities that you might not like to do but that serve your long-term vision. For example, if humility is part of your vision, you will be more likely to trade in your pride and your desire to always be right for the opportunity to serve others. Or if you aim to be a top salesperson, you'll be more willing to make prospecting calls even if you find them time-consuming and tedious.

As I've mentioned, most people think short-term and limit themselves by only performing activities they enjoy. People with vision, however, think long-term. They are willing to do activities they consider difficult or unappealing to achieve their long-term goals.

Ron's Vision Board

STRATEGY THREE: CLARIFY YOUR VISION

TOOL #3: YOUR VISION STATEMENT

One way to crystallize your vision—after writing your "be-do-haves" and making a vision board—is to create a vision statement.

A personal vision statement will help you codify your vision for your life and articulate your destiny and why you were put on this planet.

Here's my vision statement: "I live my life to empower people, rise above adversity, overcome fear, and know what it truly means to serve others. Through a lifelong commitment to be the example, I will do my best to lead others, just as my Creator leads me."

To help craft your vision statement, look back on your "be-do-have" lists and the vision board you created. What is your vision statement?

Your vision statement: _____

_____

_____

_____

_____

Remember that vision isn't just limited to individuals. You can create a vision statement with your family, your company, or people who share your spiritual beliefs, such as friends from your church or synagogue.

If you write a vision statement for your family, you and your partner may come up with your family's core values—the things you believe in as a family unit. For example, your family might be committed to respect, kindness, faith, trust, and community service. That's part of your family's vision. Then you can teach those values to your children as well.

You can also use this as a great exercise for your company's leadership team. Working within the company's core values, your team can come up with a vision statement that guides your work. At Southwestern Coaching, we encourage the entrepreneurial business leaders we coach to create a company creed and the people in management to create departmental creeds for their team. A creed is a document encapsulating a company's vision, mission, values, and principles.

The Southwestern Consulting Creed lists a number of things that we believe in and strive to live by. We review and revise the creed periodically to ensure it still supports our vision. You can read our creed on the following pages.

We've even created a Southwestern Consulting Leadership Pact, which encourages our leaders to not only uphold the company's vision but also elevate their own vision and sales efforts so they can be an example and motivation to their teams. This role-specific vision statement encourages such responsibilities as recruiting, fiscal responsibility, professionalism, planning, and openness to feedback.

STRATEGY THREE: CLARIFY YOUR VISION

THE SOUTHWESTERN CONSULTING CREED

At Southwestern Consulting, we are based on 160-year-old principles. Our vision is to be the leader in personal and professional development, creating positive impact worldwide. Our mission and the reason we exist is to help people achieve their goals in life.

As part of that pursuit, we believe in:

- Promoting the Southwestern story and its companies' philosophies to the world
- Being for what's right rather than who's right
- Promoting principles more than personalities
- Practicing what we preach
- Great leaders being great recruiters
- Seeing people not only for who they are but for who they can become
- Teaching people how to live ethically, honestly, and without shortcuts
- Laughter and helping others to laugh
- Establishing a long-term relationship with each company and every person with whom we come in contact
- Making Southwestern Consulting a place of transformation from the inside out for our clients and our team members

- Creating comprehensive internal training systems for our team members
- Challenging ourselves to continually learn, grow, innovate, and improve
- Giving the world valuable information for free as a way of introducing ourselves and earning trust
- Taking action and implementing suggestions that come from our clients and our team members
- Striving to live with integrity, self-discipline, and passion in every area of our lives

Above all, we are committed to building a company that creates a lasting legacy by building people. We are proud to represent Southwestern Family of Companies. We will work continually toward positively changing lives by investing in people, inspiring growth, and creating meaningful impact IN THE WORLD!

Having a vision statement, written out and posted where you can see it every day, is a powerful tool that can help you achieve your goals. A vision statement is proof that you believe your life has purpose. It can give you the strength and endurance to fulfill your goals, especially when you face struggles.

STRATEGY THREE: CLARIFY YOUR VISION

A VISION THAT CHANGES THE WORLD

People sometimes ask me if it's possible to have focus, ownership, and vision and still live a balanced life. I reply that a "balanced life" doesn't exist. No one doing anything great in this world is "balanced."

Everything happens in seasons. Understanding what period of life you're in will help you focus. Sometimes you have to intentionally "unbalance" certain areas of your life so you can pursue a vision that changes the world.

For instance, some people might think my running regimen is extreme. I often train in the early morning hours before my family wakes up, and I run between twenty-two and fifty miles or more most weeks. This can take anywhere from three to fourteen hours, depending on the event that I am training for. I have many reasons why I run, whether I'm crossing the mountains, forests, and trails near my home, or even the Grand Canyon. All these *whys* give me the fuel and vision I need to tackle my ultrarunning goals:

I run because God has given me a body to use, strengthen, and explore. I never want to take my body for granted.

I run because nothing tests me mentally in quite the same way. When I'm prepping for an ultrarunning event, I carefully plan my workouts, study the course and the terrain, consider the weather, and plan what nutrients to pack along the way.

I run because I want to live out the principles I speak, coach, and write about.

I run because it reminds me of how capable I am. Sometimes I'm fearful when I run—for example, when I get lost on a trail or am not adequately prepared for a big run—but I know I can push through that fear and conquer it.

I run because it helps me develop grit and thicker skin. I often feel defeated, but I always bounce back. This reassures me that nothing can take my joy and peace.

I run because it introduces me to new parts of myself. Running long distances pushes me to tap into something bigger than myself—something that would have otherwise been buried.

I run because I love seeing the beauty of the landscape that God has created—and I want to witness it in person, not onscreen.

I run because doing so reminds me how big and complex the world is. I feel connected, amazed, respectful, and even a little overwhelmed by nature when I'm on the trails.

I run because I love the sense of calm I feel after "unplugging" and going off the grid.

I run because it helps me to regain perspective of the things that truly matter and to release the things that don't.

I run because I want to live as boldly as I can.

I run because I need to be humbled and challenged on a regular basis. Running teaches me to live out the RAFT principle: When I inevitably face obstacles or setbacks, I must realize what's happening. For example, maybe I need to acknowledge that I'm way behind where I should be at a certain point on the trail. Then I accept the challenge and take ownership of the problem. Maybe I didn't train hard enough, and I need to turn around before it gets too late. Finally, I decide to focus on what I can control so I can overcome the challenges next time and ultimately be transformed.

STRATEGY THREE: CLARIFY YOUR VISION

Running is not the point, but it's a great example of where the *why* shows up in daily living.

As we reach the end of this chapter, I want to point out that vision completes one of the formulas in this book. Focus, which was the topic of chapter 1, and ownership, the topic of chapter 2, combine to create vision.

Focus + ownership = vision.

How does this work? First, you master the ability to focus—to concentrate and eliminate distractions. Next, you own your situation, your abilities, your emotions, and your strengths. Then, you clarify your vision, bringing it into focus and making it your fuel.

Your vision is your calling. Your vision is something you will pursue your whole life. It's the reason you are on this earth—it is literally what you were created for and why you were born. You're here, reading this book for a purpose. Now it's time for you to carry out that vision.

POWER STATEMENTS

Here are some affirmations on vision:

"My ability to overcome challenges at work or at home is directly tied to the clarity of my vision."

"I know exactly what I want out of life and how to get it."

"Vision is the fuel that propels me forward."

"I inspire other people with my vision."

"I'm living out my calling; I'm right where I should be."

"I've got a vision for my life, and I won't let anything hold me back."

"I'm prioritizing the activities that will help me achieve my goals."

"I see myself having a successful business and authentic, loving relationships."

"I claim the joyful future that I have envisioned."

_____
_____
_____
_____
_____
_____
_____
_____
_____
_____

STRATEGY THREE: CLARIFY YOUR VISION

SPOTLIGHT ON STRATEGY THREE:

Virgie Sandford Clarifies Her Vision

Virgie Sandford, a top sales manager with Southwestern Advantage, was raised in Spearfish, South Dakota, by a family who taught her the importance of integrity, faith, hard work, and serving others. Yet she had never been exposed to the concept of *vision*.

She learned about it in college when she joined the Southwestern Advantage program. Selling was far out of her comfort zone. "I was a shy, small-town freshman who knew nothing about sales," she said. "In fact, I had worked my whole life to avoid rejection, so the idea of selling door-to-door was intimidating." But Virgie believed in the company's vision of building skills and character in young people, so she set aside her fears and spent several successful years selling educational products for Southwestern Advantage.

After college, Virgie stayed with the company because she wanted to provide other students the same opportunity she had been given at a pivotal stage in life. She and her sales manager decided she would move to Texas, where she didn't know anyone, to start a division of the company. The same week Virgie moved, however, her sales manager unexpectedly left Southwestern Advantage. "I had to remind myself why I had chosen this work in the first place," she said. "I still believed in our program's vision and knew I could grow here. When we are clear on our 'why' and our vision, it helps us weather life's disruptions and disappointments."

In 2005, Virgie had a much more serious disruption: a near-fatal car accident. She spent eleven days in a coma, suffering serious internal injuries and broken bones, and her foot was scheduled for amputation. Over the next few months, she worked daily to relearn to read, rebuild her memory, and be able to walk again. Skilled surgeons, prayer, a positive mindset, and a commitment to her vision helped Virgie to piece her mind and body back together. Virgie felt like she was given a second chance at life, and she became committed to spiritual growth as an important part of her personal vision.

She returned to work just six months later. The transition was more difficult than she anticipated. She struggled—her team shrank from 150 people in 2005 to 60 people in 2007—but with support from her loved ones, she reframed her vision, grew her sales organization, and became a top regional sales director. Over time, Virgie further developed her personal vision to be a "lighthouse" for others. "A lighthouse helps guide people to their goals," she explained. "I want to be a

STRATEGY THREE: CLARIFY YOUR VISION

constant source of love, light, and truth for others."

In 2019, Virgie wanted objective guidance from someone who could help her fulfill her personal and professional goals. She hired Emmie Brown, one of Southwestern Consulting's executive-level coaches, because Virgie knew if she were *paying* for the advice, she would be much more likely to adopt it. Emmie challenged Virgie to more clearly identify her vision—which Virgie prioritized in order as faith, family, health, and work—and to build into her schedule specific activities related to each.

One of Virgie's family priorities was to maintain a close relationship with each of her fifteen nieces and nephews. She realized that this commitment required more than just an occasional trip to visit them in South Dakota, so she shifted her travel schedule to fly to South Dakota nearly every month and decided to start a 529 college savings plan for every child. She also finances "Travel with Aunt Virgie" trips with each child when they are in middle school, and then for high school and college graduations. This has given her an opportunity to teach her nieces and nephews to build their own vision. "Even when they are in elementary school," said Virgie, "we talk about where they might want to travel for college graduation. They can pick anywhere in the world for that trip!"

Virgie's vision evolved over time. It started with latching onto a corporate vision that she believed in. Then she created one for her own organization, developed one for her life, and began helping others create a vision for their lives as well. "Vision has to include things outside of work and possessions," said Virgie. "At the end of our life, that nice car won't be holding our hand. It will be the relationships that we have invested in that matter."

[STRATEGY FOUR]

Strengthen Your Belief System

"A person often becomes what he believes himself to be. . . . [I]f I have the belief that I can do it, I shall surely acquire the capacity to do it, even if I may not have it at the beginning."
—Mahatma Gandhi, social activist and leader of India's passive resistance movement

When I hit rock bottom during my divorce, I was able to pick myself up because I had done a lot of internal work . . . but I was able to *stay* in that positive headspace in large part because of my friend John Dammarell.

John is one of my three lifelong mentors, and he has the most solid belief system of anyone I know. A pastor and the executive director of a nonprofit (where I serve on the board), John guided me through my divorce and helped me to reset my life. He's been there for me through Van's cancer and every major event that has come my way since we met.

Mutual friends introduced us in 2013. "More than anyone," they said, "John can understand the pain you're going through." They were right. In all my years, I've never known anyone who has experienced so much pain and loss.

John went bankrupt during America's savings and loan crisis in the late 1980s and lost his home, his car, and his dog—all in six months. A devoted family man, he experienced two unwanted divorces. After that, both his adult children nearly died. In 2011, John's son, David, suffered a stroke from an acute arterial occlusion, an artery blockage in his neck that doctors said would prevent him from ever walking or talking again. (David has since miraculously recovered about 80 percent of his functioning.) Then just one month after David's stroke, John's daughter, Christie, had a life-threatening brain aneurism and a stroke in one day. Christie's health initially stabilized, but the night before she was supposed to come home from the hospital, she had a major brain bleed. Christie's husband, Richard, was forced to decide whether Christie should have a surgery that would keep her alive but permanently unresponsive, or if he should withhold medical intervention and let his wife pass away. Richard chose surgery, and John continues to visit Christie in a care facility where she has been on life support for more than a decade.

If there was ever someone who could feel justified in being bitter or who might feel crippled from trauma or want to hide, it is John. But John is the most grateful, positive, generous person I have ever met. He shows up for people, giving hours of his time and energy to nearly anyone who needs it. He doesn't complain about

STRATEGY FOUR: STRENGTHEN YOUR BELIEF SYSTEM

his trials. Instead, he encourages everyone he comes across—from strangers in the grocery store to visitors he meets at church.

John doesn't have some special DNA that magically gives him a positive outlook; he admits that he lived in bitterness and anger for many years. It wasn't until he tapped into his belief system that he was finally able to move forward.

Decades ago, John realized that even though he believed in forgiveness, he wasn't offering it to others. He started living out what he believes, and now he meticulously guards his belief system from negative thoughts and people. In addition to believing in forgiveness, John believes there is a greater purpose for his pain. He feels confident that God will work out the trials in his life for good (see Romans 8:28). To John, God is faithful no matter what. This belief helps him to persevere during tough times and move past his pain.

John lives generously because he believes God put him on this earth to help others. His belief system makes it possible for him to show up and support everyone he knows who is going through a crisis—even while he faces his own daughter's condition with positivity and hope.

WHAT DO YOU BELIEVE?

Like John's, your own belief system comprises the principles and values that are hardwired into who you are. You may have devout spiritual beliefs, such as an unwavering belief in God or a belief in a higher power. Or you might believe in love, family, or helping those in need.

When you have strong beliefs—whatever they are—you have strong convictions. When you have strong convictions, you have unwavering confidence. When you have unwavering confidence, you can do bold things. And when you act boldly, you get results. Having a strong sense of belief can help you break through limits and redefine what's possible for you.

I often remind myself, "Limits begin where belief ends." To paraphrase Zig Ziglar, it's not the height of your logic but the depth of your convictions—your belief system—that matters most. Belief helps you to be innovative and challenge the status quo. When your beliefs fuel your actions, you have the energy to do more, the ability to remain positive, and the drive to help the people around you see what they are truly capable of doing too.

Unfortunately, some people don't have beliefs that support growth. They may believe their life doesn't have purpose or that they are unimportant. Maybe something traumatic happened in their past or they just absorbed negative messages from society. Either way, these people feel limited. That isn't their reality, though; those limits exist only in their mind. And those limits can be changed by having a strong belief system.

Having the ability to believe in yourself starts at a young age. For example, children aren't born knowing how to swim. They usually start by learning how to blow bubbles in the water. Then they learn to dog paddle and swim different strokes. Over time, they are able to dive into the deep end, swim to the surface, and reach the edge of the pool. But children learn to swim not just because they have been instructed in the proper techniques—they

STRATEGY FOUR: STRENGTHEN YOUR BELIEF SYSTEM

do it because they believe it's possible to move through water and stay afloat.

Children pick up things more easily than adults because they haven't yet learned that they can't do something. Unfortunately, as we age, society often conditions us to place limiting beliefs on who we are and what we can do. In high school, we're told that a four-year college is the only way to succeed in life. In college, we're encouraged to work a traditional, nine-to-five corporate job. As adults, we watch commercials that tell us that driving certain cars or trucks will show our neighbors that we've "made it."

If we're not careful, we'll center our beliefs and make decisions based on what society tells us to do.

What is your belief system? Is it constructive or destructive? How do you approach life? As a coach, I get to hear people's unfiltered thoughts daily. Some people believe that everything happens for a reason and that their life has purpose. Others believe that life is just hard, and everyone is out to get them. This negative belief system, that people are toxic and the world is a terrible place, shows up everywhere on social media through memes that are meant to be funny but instead are a sad commentary on our cynical culture.

In my coaching work, I've found that many people float through life, letting everybody else construct their belief system. They let social media or the news tell them how things should be, and most of the beliefs they do have are fickle instead of solid. Some of these people use society's labels to describe their belief system—for example, they call themselves a conservative or a liberal, an atheist or an agnostic. But beliefs are much more than labels. Labels are limiting, whether you are calling yourself introverted or extroverted, a cynic or a fan, a math person or a creative person. For beliefs to really make a difference, they must be strong and well formed. They must come from your own value system and be shaped by your own convictions and experiences—not from society, other people, or external labels.

Ultimately, your belief system guides your decision-making, driving what you do or don't do. Having strong, positive beliefs is at the heart of innovative work. Beliefs enable you to be in touch with what's possible, know your own barriers, be honest about your goals, and stay positive even if you get derailed.

Identifying your beliefs and then shifting negative ones into positive ones is a foundation for redefining possible.

BEWARE OF BARRIERS

Before you can use your beliefs to redefine possible, you must first make sure you are thinking with complete freedom. To do that, you need to be aware of belief barriers.

Belief barriers are assumptions that limit the action you would take to accomplish a goal. Limiting beliefs can play out in many ways, affecting how we budget, the way we accrue credit card debt, how—and whether—we ask for a raise, and how we approach relationships. Belief barriers might include thoughts that affect your work, such as, "I'll never make more money," "I don't have the right experience," or "No one's going to listen to what I have to say." They might include thoughts that impact your relationships, like, "I'm not good enough to date that person" or

STRATEGY FOUR: STRENGTHEN YOUR BELIEF SYSTEM

"I'm socially awkward; no one likes me."

You probably have beliefs that are not serving your best interests. When you can identify those negative beliefs, then you have taken the first step to reprogram those beliefs. It's amazing what happens once our belief barriers are knocked down. I used to think a three-mile run was long, but once my beliefs changed about what I could do, I worked up to running one hundred miles at once!

If you line up ten people with the same amount of talent, you will see dramatically different results because of their varying belief barriers. Some of the people simply won't believe as big as others. But I'd bet every day of the week on the person who believes biggest. In fact, my coaching practice is built upon the belief that every person is unique and can change—no matter who they are. Although I don't know for certain who said it, I love this quote and cite it often: "If you think you can or you think you can't, you're right."

The good news is that you can overcome your belief barriers. Start by challenging your beliefs. First, identify a personal belief barrier you want to demolish this month. Look at your vision board for your big goals and identify one thing that's not happening.

For instance, let's say your vision board includes a picture of a triathlon medal. Your goal is to compete in your first triathlon, but you've never done the swimming portion of the race. "I'm a great runner and cyclist," you tell yourself, "but I'm a weak swimmer. Maybe I should stick to marathons and bike rides instead." To break this belief barrier, you must shift from focusing on what you haven't done (competitive swimming) to reminding yourself that you are a strong, well-trained athlete.

Whichever belief barrier you choose to break, make sure it's one that stretches your abilities. Do something that intimidates you. Change your self-talk. Train hard to beat your own personal records. Then make it happen.

LIVING WITHOUT BELIEF BARRIERS

Once you get rid of belief barriers, the sky's the limit.

The best possible example of someone who breaks belief barriers is my colleague Henry Bedford, CEO and chairman of the board at Southwestern Family of Companies. Henry's belief in what's possible is off the charts.

Henry Bedford started his nearly fifty-year career with Southwestern as a college student, selling door-to-door with Southwestern Advantage. He was then hired by the company in 1976 as an internal auditor. At the time, Southwestern consisted of one company and one start-up called Nashville Educational Marketing Services, with total combined revenues of $25 million. Now, as of 2024, Southwestern Family of Companies consists of more than twenty-five companies across over twenty countries and millions of customers worldwide—and Henry has been personally involved in acquiring and/or developing every single one of those new businesses. He learned from his mentors that if you run a company by the right beliefs and principles, you can figure anything out.

Henry's amazing belief extends to his personal life. He has

STRATEGY FOUR: STRENGTHEN YOUR BELIEF SYSTEM

skydived more than five hundred times, including doing skydives out of hot-air balloons. He owns a hot-air balloon and has competed in and won international competitions.

From there, he got into riding motorcycles during his vacations. He started with one motorcycle, which he rode from the East Coast to the West Coast of the United States, then from Los Angeles up through Canada and Alaska, continuing each year from wherever he left the bike the year before. He bought another motorcycle in Los Angeles and rode with a friend south through Mexico into Central America, across the Panama Canal, and down into South America, leaving his bike at the end of each journey, usually in the home or barn of a local he had befriended. He continued through Colombia, Ecuador, and Peru, riding his motorcycle over the Andes on goat trails or often with no road at all, and into the Amazon.

After that, Henry took up sailing. He bought a forty-two-foot sailboat, despite the fact that he had never sailed a large boat in his life, and taught himself how to sail by watching YouTube videos. He sailed through the open seas to Cuba, Grand Cayman, and then to Panama.

Henry also believes in helping others, a principle he says he learned from his mentor and former Southwestern CEO Ralph Mosley. Over his career, Henry has found time to build Safe Haven Family Shelter in Nashville, Tennessee; has led the building of homes for needy families in the US, Mexico, and Guatemala; and has raised money to help North Korean refugees escape to freedom.

Henry is a great example that your belief can take you anywhere when you have a clear vision. What are your goals and passions? If you don't have a clear answer to the question, it's okay. The answer will emerge. I like to compare this process to a scene in the movie *The Last Samurai*. In the film, Katsumoto (played by Ken Watanabe) asks, "You believe a man can change his destiny?"

Tom Cruise's character, Nathan Algren, replies, "I think a man does what he can until his destiny is revealed."[16]

CHANGE IS PROGRESS

All of us believe in our gut that it's possible to do things we don't yet know how to do.

For example, if you play a sport, you didn't automatically know the rules of the game or the technique of how to play. You probably practiced, joined a team, or took lessons. But because you believed that you could play tennis or hockey or golf, you figured it out. Similarly, you weren't born knowing how to write research papers or solve complex math equations like you did in high school or college. Instead, you worked hard, studied, asked questions, and believed that you would eventually learn the skills required.

The point is, there are very few things that we just "know" how to do in life. Everything else comes through a lot of hard work, some natural skill, and having the confidence—the sheer belief—that we will be able to learn new things.

When you're starting to make a big change, setbacks will happen, whether you are learning how to manage your company's financials or just climbing on your bike for a workout. You might

STRATEGY FOUR: STRENGTHEN YOUR BELIEF SYSTEM

catch yourself thinking, "I'm no good at spreadsheets," "Man, I hate doing that exercise," or "I'm terrible at speaking in front of people."

Resist the impulse. Don't beat yourself up or indulge in negative beliefs. You'll just revert back to your old ways, and you definitely don't want to do that.

I have mentioned self-talk in other chapters of this book, but this is where it is truly crucial, because your beliefs literally reprogram your life. We have a saying at Southwestern: "Success comes from our actions; actions come from our feelings; feelings come from our attitudes; attitudes come from our beliefs; and beliefs are who we are."

At the beginning of this book, I talked about how our leadership team steered Southwestern Consulting through the early months of the COVID-19 pandemic. The news at the time was doom and gloom, with stories about how the stock market was crashing and companies were being forced to furlough employees. It would have been easy to get caught up in that cycle of fear. But our team believed completely in our work at Southwestern Consulting—in fact, we believed that our mission of impact was even more critical during the crisis than it ever had been, and that motivated us to take action.

If I had given in to that fear and lost sight of my beliefs, I probably wouldn't have finished writing this book you're holding right now.

As you can see, your beliefs are an important ingredient in achieving success. Beliefs come from your programming and conditioning. What you think about all day is what you will believe. What you read and watch also influences your beliefs, so if you struggle with belief barriers, I recommend studying books like the Bible, reading inspiring biographies, watching motivational TED Talks, or listening to podcasts like *The Action Catalyst*.

Your belief barriers will slowly start to dissolve when you examine your self-talk. Notice those victories and build on them. Catch yourself doing things right! Your success will compound if you build yourself up. Consider adding affirmations to support the progress you've made toward your goal and to help keep you accountable.

Finally, be aware of how you're feeling. You will inevitably hit a point where a challenge pops up and derails you. When that happens, you'll need something—like an affirmation or a helpful podcast—to keep you going. You can also try using the RAFT technique.

Don't be deterred. Look for progress, not perfection. Remember, this is not supposed to be easy. You need faith, perseverance to overcome, and affirmations that speak to your resilience. Forgive yourself, move on, and keep believing.

BELIEVE BIG AND CHANGE YOUR LIFE

When we burst through belief barriers, set big goals, and tackle them with gusto, we are building confidence that we can handle anything in life. And sometimes, when we are facing difficult things, we need that confidence more than ever.

I was sitting with my son Van in the hospital one day during a chemo treatment when I felt tears start to roll down my cheeks.

STRATEGY FOUR: STRENGTHEN YOUR BELIEF SYSTEM

Between Van's battle against leukemia, my new marriage (Desireé and I hadn't even gone on our honeymoon yet!), our two other kids at home, and my responsibilities at work, I was overwhelmed. But I didn't want my son to see me break down. I wanted to be strong in front of him and show Van that, as a family, we could all rise above any obstacle that came our way.

I also wanted to show him what it meant to take true ownership of my beliefs. I've always believed that life is full of highs and lows. Challenges are part of everyone's story. I also believe that my circumstances are not what defines me—it's how I respond to those circumstances that makes the difference. So, at the height of Van's crisis, I decided that I would not get caught up in beliefs that made me a victim or shifted blame. I believed that this part of my story would be used for good. I vowed to live out my beliefs so I could be the best father, husband, and coach possible and guide my family through this crisis.

One of the things I did was set a big goal at work. My hand was shaky as I wrote it out. Even though I was behind in my sales goals because I had been at the hospital so much, I vowed to break the company's all-time record for the most client sales in a year and become a senior partner by the end of 2017.

This turned out to be an even bigger challenge than I'd anticipated. I doubted myself nearly every day. I was constantly on the verge of giving up and had a lot of strong rationalizations for why I should let go of my goal. But I followed my plan. I tried not to make excuses. I kept to a strict schedule, staying focused and working my heart out when I was at the office, and then shutting off my phone and filling my heart again when I was with my family. I spoke affirmations, telling myself, "Just stick to the plan. If this goal is in my heart, it must be true; it must be pure."

After my last workshop of the year in mid-December, I wasn't sure if I could reach my goal. I told a close friend, "I might have a shot to break the previous record, but I think one of our other coaches has done more."

I was starting to give up. "Maybe it wasn't meant to be," I said. "Maybe I should just go home, be with my family, and get ready to celebrate the new year. I can always try again next year." But my friend reminded me, "Finish strong. You never know what can happen."

I didn't want to break that record just to beat some number. I wanted to do it to change more lives! So, I looked at the wall in my office, where I had the faces of the people I coached posted prominently. I reminded myself that those people were fighting to improve their own lives. Even more exciting, I believed I was there to help them do it.

On December 29—the last business day of the year—I did it. I broke the record by signing up one more coaching client. That one day, that one extra call, that one client made the difference, enabling me to break the company record and finish number one on a team of top-producing salespeople. More important, I was able to be that example of belief for my three kids.

STRATEGY FOUR: STRENGTHEN YOUR BELIEF SYSTEM

POWER STATEMENTS

These affirmations will help you see yourself as someone who has a solid belief system. You can use these affirmations to retrain your brain to burst through belief barriers and accomplish greater things than you ever imagined:

"I can. I will. End of story."

"I believe in myself and trust the process."

"I can do this."

"I've done it before, and I can do it again."

"I believe I can change the course of my life."

"I let go of all doubts."

"I cut through belief barriers like a warrior clearing a path in the jungle."

"I choose to believe in the good. I set aside negative thoughts that don't serve me."

SPOTLIGHT ON STRATEGY FOUR:

WILL BARTHOLOMEW EXPANDS HIS BELIEFS

As a collegiate football player, Will Bartholomew seemed destined for a career in the National Football League. At the University of Tennessee, he played fullback behind legendary quarterback Peyton Manning. His team won the national championship in 1998, and he was captain as a senior. Along the way, Will captured a number of NCAA Southeastern Conference honors.

In 2001, he signed a contract to play for the Denver Broncos as an undrafted free agent. Then, in one moment on the practice field, he suffered a severe knee injury that sent him home to Nashville to recover. He would never again play professional sports—but a new path opened up for him.

During his recovery, Will realized, "There was nowhere for me to train like I did when I was playing for a Division I college team." So he decided to fill the need himself. He bought some equipment and opened a facility called D1 Training. Other athletes were showing an interest in his program, and his success was growing . . . but he realized he needed help scaling the business to the size he envisioned. At the time, D1 was a small operation with four gyms, but Will knew it

STRATEGY FOUR: STRENGTHEN YOUR BELIEF SYSTEM

could be nationwide one day. That's when he contacted Southwestern Coaching, and our team came on board to help Will put sales processes in place to grow the business.

Soon, Will's entire team was on board too. After spending a month observing how D1 went about a number of critical functions—from sales to team recruitment to training—Southwestern Coaching identified several areas in need of improvement. First, while Will had spent a lot of time developing world-class training services and programs, he knew he needed help to get a sales process in place so he could get new clients and hit revenue goals. Will's coach created a number of selling and recruiting systems, processes, training manuals, and scripts to make the sales and recruiting operations more efficient and more effective, and then reverse-engineered D1's goals into the daily activities that would be necessary to meet them.

For example, his coach discovered that to recruit just one new athlete customer, a team member would have to spend three hours at a sporting goods store developing at least twenty leads, then follow up with phone calls to get just three people to come to the gym. From those three, one person would enroll. So the team at Southwestern Coaching helped set up critical success factors—tracking systems that would recognize and reward sales and prospecting leaders.

The bigger issue, however, was trickier to address: the whole D1 team—including Will himself—was being held back by belief barriers. Early on, Will had decided to hire team members who were athletes because they understood sports training. The problem was, they didn't yet understand sales. For many, it shook their confidence and belief in their ability to succeed outside of athletics.

To combat this corrosive doubt, Will's coach worked on correcting D1's negative self-talk. As he explained to the D1 team members, what you tell yourself about your abilities determines your reality. More than just teaching hard skills like sales scripts and processes, he shared positive affirmations for each person to use to break their belief barriers so they could believe they would be just as successful at sales as they'd been at their sport.

Southwestern Coaching trained the D1 team on what true professional selling is all about, explaining that true salesmanship is about helping people, identifying a need, and filling the need. Will's coach helped D1 focus on asking questions, listening, and customizing their presentation to the needs of their prospect.

Once the team members had broken those belief barriers and better understood what it meant to be a sales professional, they were ready to embrace learning

STRATEGY FOUR: STRENGTHEN YOUR BELIEF SYSTEM

new skills, just like they had done as rookie athletes.

The coach created competitive incentives, weekly and monthly competitions, and daily and weekly technical trainings. Soon D1's belief in what was possible changed as they began to organically grow their sales revenues and became true sales professionals.

One small victory at a time, D1 revamped the company culture and learned to believe they could accomplish whatever they set out to do. When Will hired Southwestern Coaching, D1 was a small business with four locations. Today, D1 Training is franchised and has reached more than two million people total, including 100 NFL draft picks, 1,000 professional athletes, and 2,000 collegiate athletes. The company trains more than 100,000 scholastic athletes each year.

[STRATEGY FIVE]

Cultivate Confidence

> *"You gain strength, courage, and confidence by every experience in which you really stop to look fear in the face. ... You must do the thing you think you cannot do."*
> —Eleanor Roosevelt, First Lady, writer, and advocate

Few things will shake your confidence faster than teetering on the edge of heatstroke at the bottom of the Grand Canyon, nine miles and six thousand feet of elevation away from help. Especially when you know you have only yourself to blame.

But that's getting ahead of the story.

I have been an athlete my whole life. As a kid, I played every team sport available. When I got older, I could usually be found at the gym or city park, hustling in pickup games or on some recreational league team or another. Then I discovered running, and a whole new world of fitness and endurance opened up for me. In the beginning, I wasn't fast and couldn't run very far. But I kept training and eventually competed in marathons and triathlons. I loved the runner's high and the sense of achievement I felt when crossing a finish line.

Then, after my divorce, a buddy and I took up trail running, covering distances I didn't think were possible just a few years earlier. Drew and I started with a fifty-kilometer run, then stepped up to fifty miles and even a hundred miles at a time, through some of the country's most beautiful scenery.

Drew and I have trained together for a long time, so when we decided to complete the famous Rim-to-Rim-to-Rim run in the Grand Canyon, we were confident we'd succeed. The course was a "mere" forty-seven miles—from the South Rim down to the Colorado River in the canyon floor, up to the North Rim, and back again. That meant a cumulative elevation change of twenty-four thousand feet, but we were sure our extensive training would more than prepare us for it. I added pictures of the canyon to my vision board and dreamed of the day I could cross off the run on my list of goals.

Our plan was to run in April, but because of a few personal delays, we didn't go out until the end of June. That was mistake number one! That midsummer day in 2016, Drew and I descended from the South Rim at 5:00 a.m. on a desert morning. Our plan was to be back where we started by 7:00 p.m. that evening, fourteen grueling but satisfying hours later. It took only three hours for us to fall behind that pace and to suspect we'd grossly miscalculated the magnitude of our undertaking. By noon, the temperature in the canyon was 114 degrees, with an apparent heat index of 140. There was no shade. We made it to the bottom of the canyon, struggling

STRATEGY FIVE: CULTIVATE CONFIDENCE

with shooting pain in our legs from severe cramps. Other than a couple of rafters floating down the river, no other people were in sight. Drew and I started the next leg of the journey, up to the North Rim, but by 2:00 p.m. we could no longer deny we were in real trouble. Just three miles from the top, we decided to turn back, knowing we should have done so miles earlier.

We were suffering from severe heat exhaustion. We could barely breathe, and we couldn't lower our heart rate, even with resting. Then the vomiting set in. Nothing we ate or drank stayed in our stomach more than a minute, and muscle cramps kept us from moving at more than a snail's pace. I can honestly say I had never been more afraid for my life. It took nine hours for us to inch our way from the river back to the South Rim. We reached our car at 3:00 a.m., twenty-two hours after we'd left it with such high hopes.

Unbelievably, the physical trauma I suffered that day wasn't the worst part of the ordeal—it was the realization that I had failed. I flew home, feeling defeated. Everyone we'd told about our adventure would know how foolish and shortsighted we had been. I worried that I would come across as a fraud. How could I continue inspiring life-changing confidence in others when mine had been shattered so thoroughly?

ARE YOU BASING YOUR CONFIDENCE ON THE RIGHT THING?

Confidence can make you feel like you can move mountains, or even run them, but the wrong kind of confidence won't take you very far.

Merriam-Webster defines confidence as "the state of being certain."[17] In my coaching business, I like to describe confidence as the authentic expression of having certainty and belief in what you are doing and how you are moving toward your goals. With confidence, you can take bold action. You can move decisively with purpose. There's one important caveat: when I describe confidence, I do not mean cockiness. Confidence that turns into arrogance will hurt your business and relationships. The key to avoiding ego is getting feedback, since we are all a work in progress. This will help rewire and reprogram your thoughts. (See chapter 2 for more insight on feedback.)

There are three types of confidence: false, conditional, and unconditional.

False confidence: With false confidence, people talk a big game. They describe all the great things they could do, but they are full of excuses for why they never actually do them. Then, after the fact, they say, "I should have," "I could have," or "I would have." False confidence can also be seen in negative self-talk. People might have a smile on their face and say, "Oh, things are going fine. Today's a great day." But when they look in the mirror, they feel like a loser who can't get anything right.

Everybody has false confidence at some point. We've all had to "fake it 'til we make it," no matter who we are. But it's the worst place to be because it's when our confidence is the shakiest.

Conditional confidence: When I first ran the Rim-to-Rim-to-Rim, I was the picture of conditional confidence: I had based my self-worth on attaining a particular result.

STRATEGY FIVE: CULTIVATE CONFIDENCE

Most people struggle with this. If you have a big day, a big month, or a big quarter—for example, if you've successfully rolled out a product launch or gotten kudos from your boss on a completing a huge, complicated project—then you might hold your head high and feel good about yourself. But if you have a day, week, or year where you don't hit your sales goals or you don't see the results from your advertising campaign, you might feel "less than."

Conditional confidence is not just seen in the professional world—it's part of life. People often attach their self-worth to getting specific results, including results they can't control. For instance, couples who want to get pregnant will sometimes feel they are less worthy in society's eyes if they cannot conceive. Or people who struggle with their weight may only feel good about themselves if they have reached a certain number on the scale.

Unconditional confidence: If we're going to redefine possible, we must replace our false or conditional confidence with unconditional confidence. At Southwestern Coaching, we've worked with tens of thousands of clients over the years, and in our experience, the most successful people all share unconditional confidence.

Unconditional confidence is the best kind of confidence, because it is based on your beliefs and habits. With unconditional confidence, you are aware that sometimes you'll do well and sometimes you won't. You know that your pain and your struggles are temporary. You understand that if you stay focused on your beliefs and stick to your habits, you will persevere. You just don't quit. And you find that you have faith, which eliminates fear. (I'll talk more about faith in the next chapter.)

But what does it actually mean to have unconditional confidence? It means having confidence without conditions—without thinking, "I'll feel confident if this happens."

When you have unconditional confidence, you wake up every day focused on your life purpose and mission. You don't worry about what others think of you; instead, you focus on offering grace and love. You operate without conditions, and you serve other people without having an agenda. You are authentic and peaceful, knowing that in this moment you are and have everything you need.

Let's look at three key steps to gaining unconditional confidence.

STEP #1: START BY LETTING GO

When you have unconditional confidence, you let go of things you can't control. Instead, you focus on the three things you can control: your attitude, which includes your beliefs and self-talk; your activities or habits; and your schedule.

Your attitude: I've talked a lot about attitude and self-talk in previous chapters. You can use positive self-talk and the affirmations listed at the end of each chapter to create an attitude of unconditional confidence. Your attitude is influenced by the people you surround yourself with—a concept that I'll discuss in greater detail in chapter 6. If you surround yourself with people who lift you up and believe in your hopes and dreams, your attitude will improve. If you surround yourself with people who are negative and focused on telling you why your hopes and dreams

STRATEGY FIVE: CULTIVATE CONFIDENCE

are silly, your outlook will suffer. I love this quote from motivational speaker Zig Ziglar, who often said, "Your attitude, not your aptitude, will determine your altitude."[18]

Your activities: Your activities are the actions you do every hour, every minute, and even every second of the day. Your workout routine is an activity, what you eat is an activity, and what you read is an activity. The people you choose to spend time with or decide to coach, the number of papers you grade, the amount of emails you answer—these are all activities. Going on a date night, reading a news article, and taking your child or your niece or nephew on a bike ride is an activity. The things you do that waste time are also activities, such as the amount of time you spend binge-watching TV, mindlessly scrolling through social media, drinking too much alcohol, or gossiping about your neighbors.

Oftentimes we do things without thinking. To get a handle on what fills your time, make a list of all the activities, both personal and business, that you engage in every single day. Now put a check mark next to the activities you have control over. Those activities are the ones that you have influence over and will help you reach your goals by building up unconditional confidence.

Your schedule: Although some parts of your schedule—like what time you need to be at work or when you have to drop the kids off at school—might be dictated by outside sources, most of your time is typically within your control. You determine what time you go to bed, what time you wake up, when you return a phone call and how long you talk, when you take a coffee break or go to lunch, and what time you stop working.

When you focus on your schedule, you gain control of your time. In their book *Boundaries,* authors Henry Cloud and John Townsend make the point that if you don't like how others treat your time, it's your fault.[19] I agree. Every day, through your actions and attitude, you teach the people around you how to interact with you and whether they should respect your schedule. When you focus on the things you can control, meaning your attitude, your activities, and your schedule, you stop worrying about messing up. You're not concerned about your results. Why? Because you have confidence—true confidence—born from knowing that your foundation of beliefs, skills, and habits has prepared you for any situation. You know you are doing your best.

Nate Vogel, my former manager at Southwestern Advantage and my roommate of six years, likens confidence to the metaphor of holding sand on a beach. The people you interact with every day are like grains of sand on a beach. When you hold the sand tightly, you are more attached to whether others like you, want to work with you, or choose to be your friend. The harder you grasp that sand, the more likely it is to slip between your fingers.

But when you hold the sand loosely—when you really don't care what people think, or whether they want to work with you, or if they decide to be your friend—most of the sand remains. People with unconditional confidence don't worry about what people think, and they don't have their self-worth tied up in getting results. They care less, but they get more.

This idea applies to many situations, whether you're an account executive managing a difficult client, a human resources

STRATEGY FIVE: CULTIVATE CONFIDENCE

manager giving a company-wide presentation, or a student studying for a final exam. For example, if you have an upcoming test and you stay up all night to cram, you will become frantic, tired, and overwhelmed, which makes it harder to learn. Whatever facts you manage to retain in that last-minute study session will be offset by how bad you feel when you take the test.

When you have unconditional confidence, though, you believe in your abilities, so you plan ahead and give your best effort. You focus on the things you can control, such as not waiting until the last minute to study, ensuring you get enough sleep, and keeping a good perspective. You tell yourself, "I can do this." You make and follow a study plan. You are relaxed, feeling the calmness that comes from having true confidence, and because of that you get a higher score.

STEP #2: GET THE RIGHT PERSPECTIVE

One trait you can develop that promotes unconditional confidence is perspective. When you have perspective, you understand that things are usually not as bad as they sound or as good as they may seem.

Perspective leads to confidence. Let's go back to the studying example. Some people, when faced with an important exam, think, "If I fail this test, people are going to think less of me. I won't be successful, my GPA or future career will be ruined, and I'll lose my scholarship." Those people have lost perspective. Their confidence is shaky because it's conditional.

When you have the right perspective, however, you can keep

your eyes on the big picture. You will most likely pass the test, but if you don't, you know that you'll have more opportunities in the future. One test or one "off day" won't make or break your GPA or future career because you have the perspective that you are unstoppable—a perspective that is fueled by consistent activity and positive self-talk.

Here are five ways you can develop the perspective that will help bring you unconditional confidence:

1. Identify your current default perspective.

The first step is to be aware of your current perspective. Is it already positive, or does it need some tweaking?

Perspective matters. We often adopt a specific perspective early in life—for example, believing that we are better off tackling problems alone or that we're not allowed to make mistakes—and we don't check in as adults to determine whether it still works for us. We can also get so caught up in our emotions that we quickly lose sight of perspective.

You have a choice in creating your perspective. To maintain a healthy outlook, I recommend creating perspective anchors. These are times in your life when you developed perspective. For example, did you go through a breakup or divorce only to realize that your current partner is a much better fit for you? You can look back at this event, learn from your history, and quickly remind yourself that things are going to turn out for the best.

Ask yourself, "Do I have an overall positive can-do perspective, or is my outlook negative (what a pessimist might call 'realistic')?

What is my perspective toward myself, my significant other, or my job?" When you are aware of your default reaction, you can regain perspective right away.

2. Open your mind to new perspectives.

The second step is to identify other, more positive perspectives. You may need to gather more information or educate yourself to identify and adopt a new perspective. You can do this by spending time with people who have a different point of view, reading books about gaining a positive perspective, or hiring a coach. Traveling outside your comfortable "bubble" or volunteering with people who are less fortunate can also give you a broader perspective, reminding you that your situation might not be as challenging as you thought.

One of the easiest ways to adopt a new perspective is to simply talk with friends, mentors, and coworkers who have different points of view. Avoid venting with people who already share your perspective, and actively look for opportunities to hear new ideas.

3. Experiment with new perspectives.

The third step is to play with these different perspectives. See what works for you and how that perspective will impact your life.

If your previous perspective was "I'm lazy and not very smart," then you will most likely experience depression and anxiety. Tell yourself something positive instead. Say out loud, "I'm always learning! I'm growing, I'm humble, and I'm a good person."

When you start to see yourself from a new angle, your

whole perspective shifts. You will begin to find consistent joy, not circumstantial happiness. And that speaks to unconditional, versus conditional, confidence.

4. Choose the perspective that will serve you best.

Step four is to realize that you have the ability to choose your perspective. If you tend to be negative or "realistic," you can consciously decide to be more positive. You can learn to do that through coaching, reading, self-talk, and being selective about the people you choose to associate with, particularly those you allow to influence your thinking.

A lot of what I do in my coaching program is help provide perspective. When you surround yourself with the right people, they can help change your outlook. Check in with people you trust from time to time so that you view events through the right lens. Listen to those people and be open to their feedback.

If you're consistently negative about people or events, you are probably making poor decisions. And that's when you lose confidence. When you begin to see yourself and others differently, you'll begin to build unconditional confidence.

5. Practice these positive perspectives every day.

Finally, the fifth step is to be consistent. The changes you've made need to be sustainable.

For example, you can put on an expensive new shirt and suddenly feel confident. But that's not a good long-term tactic, because tomorrow the shirt will be dirty. It will never be new

STRATEGY FIVE: CULTIVATE CONFIDENCE

again. You need sustainable principles to create lasting behavioral change, and these principles can transform you from the inside out.

Changing your perspective takes effort. Start by writing down several things you are going to work on. For example, if you want to build your confidence, list three positive things about yourself at the end of each day. This will reinforce your perspective, because you're paying attention to the things you like about yourself throughout the day.

You can also try visualization. Picture a life where you feel centered, carefree, full of joy. Imagine that when negative or bad things happen to you, you don't overreact; you simply take them in stride. You don't feel like you deserve anything, because you understand that all good things are given to you. You are simply happy to be alive, and you strive to spend your time joyfully serving others. You operate out of a perspective of thankfulness and gratitude. (If you'd like some more concrete tips on how to increase your gratitude, see Appendix B in the back of the book.)

Have regular check-ins to make sure you're sticking with your new perspective. When you're stressed, you might revert to old habits and ways of thinking. But that's normal. You can get back on track quickly.

As I've said, these tasks take work, but the payoff is mind-blowing. The lens you view the world through will transform, and you will experience positive changes. These changes will activate the reward center in your brain,[20] encouraging you to continue your hard work so you can feel those positive emotions again and again.

STEP 3: CREATE CONFIDENCE ANCHORS

Just as you can create perspective anchors, you can also establish confidence anchors.

A confidence anchor is a victory that you can revisit—a memory of a time when you redefined what was possible. For example, you might remember when you broke a personal fitness record, gave your first speech to hundreds of people, won a baseball game where the odds were stacked against your team, or conquered a fear that was holding you back at work or in your personal life. That event was a turning point, a catalyst in your history that you can trace back to and say, "After this event happened, I changed." When you leverage that event, you can catapult yourself to the next level of belief and confidence in what's possible.

Anchors are solid, strong, and immovable. They stand firm in any storm. If you haven't figured it out already, life is full of storms. If you are not currently in a storm, you can be sure that one is coming. Fortunately, confidence anchors will help you stay calm. They can literally mean the difference between living your life with peace and joy or suffering through the day with stress and anxiety.

What storms did you experience yesterday or even just this morning? Did you open an email that raised your blood pressure or get news that frightened you? We experience storms all day, every day. That's why we need confidence anchors.

Confidence anchors work because they become stepping stones. Once you've accomplished something, you know that you can accomplish even more. You can create a confidence anchor

STRATEGY FIVE: CULTIVATE CONFIDENCE

for yourself or for others. You can provide one for your whole company, giving your team an anchor to reference when times are tough. Or you can set a personal confidence anchor just by doing something new—or even better, doing something that scares you.

One thing to watch out for with confidence anchors is "peaking." You don't ever want to let yourself think that you are at your peak, or that you've "arrived." Because as soon as you've peaked, everything else is downhill. You want to avoid being like the stereotypical high school quarterback who spends his whole life retelling the same story because those were the glory days. Instead, use your confidence anchors to catapult you to the next level, where you can then find your next confidence anchor to keep moving forward.

When you leverage confidence anchors, you know that you can keep going because you have the evidence that you can succeed. You are called to do more, serve more, and touch as many people's lives as possible. Every win sets the stage for the next, and the next.

I use confidence anchors to propel my business and personal life forward. For example, when I'm facing challenges at work, I often remind myself of when the company leaders and I successfully used the RAFT technique to navigate the beginning of the COVID-19 crisis. "I helped steer our company through a global pandemic," I tell myself. "I can find a solution for this client!" (For more details on the RAFT technique, see Appendix A.)

Another one of my biggest confidence anchors comes from an experience when I failed on a grand scale . . . and then tried again.

MY PERSONAL CONFIDENCE ANCHOR

After my buddy Drew and I failed to meet our goal of running the Grand Canyon the first time, you might think we would have been hesitant to try again. It's true that my confidence was deeply shaken by how badly we missed the mark. But even before we left the South Rim parking lot that day to head home in defeat, Drew and I looked at each other and said, "We'll be back."

Five months later, in November 2016, we made good on that promise. This time when we got out of the car at 4:00 a.m. on a frosty fall morning and looked over the edge into the canyon below, we were not the same men. For one thing, that previous summer, we had trained differently, building on what we had learned. We ran at higher elevations and in warmer temperatures to acclimate. We educated ourselves about how to work through cramps and manage our body temperature more effectively.

More important, we had shed the ridiculous idea that what lay ahead would be similar to any of the runs we'd done before. Long gone was the cocky notion, "We've got this!" We also stopped defining success by how long it might take us to complete the circuit. In other words, we approached the challenge with a very different mindset—and a new kind of confidence.

I'd like to say that made all the difference, and we breezed through the course faster and easier than expected. But I can't. Even without the searing heat of summer beating on us every minute, we still vomited occasionally and had to rest our cramping muscles frequently. It took eighteen hours to arrive back where we started—four hours longer than we'd hoped. Many times through the long day we wondered if we were destined to fail again. But we didn't quit, and ultimately, we finished what we had started that June. This time, when we drove back to the airport, our exhaustion and pain were tempered by joy instead of compounded by defeat.

That's why, of all the confidence anchors I've created in my life, our completion of the Rim-to-Rim-to-Rim run is one of the most memorable and most powerful. In fact, our sense of achievement was that much sweeter for having failed the first time! When you are bold and courageous and take risks—when you just go for it with everything you've got—even "failure" can be a good thing. Allowing an experience to strengthen and refine your confidence can help you bounce back better than before.

CONFIDENCE BRINGS SUCCESS

You don't have to run forty-seven miles through the desert to find a confidence anchor. My friend and colleague Dana Potthoff's biggest confidence anchor came from the streets of New York City.

Dana is one of the most accomplished people I know. She commands the stage at speaking events and has worked with hundreds of companies across multiple industries. As a partner at Southwestern Consulting, Dana is fully confident that her life has purpose: she believes that there is a mission and vision bigger than herself.

You'd never know it, but Dana's confidence was tested early in her career. In her first significant job after college, she was employed by the world's largest custom clothier, where she opened a West Coast office, worked with many public figures, and grew the company's female clientele. However, after several years, Dana felt like there was something more for her. In a leap of faith, she quit her job with the clothier, became a coach for Southwestern Consulting, and moved to New York City.

It took time for Dana to get her new business off the ground in New York City, as she had no existing network there. She often questioned if she'd made the right choice or whether she was even good at sales. Her confidence plummeted when she got blown off during cold calls. Dana prayed, meditated, and spoke affirmations, trusting that if she did her part, the business would come. She also realized that most people were worried about what *they* were doing, not what *she* was doing. And she trusted in her vision and work. In 2015—her first full year with the company—she was named Southwestern Consulting's Coach of the Year. Dana went on to become the number one producer at Southwestern Consulting for seven consecutive years, and she won the company's Trifecta Award for selling, recruiting, and team-leading in 2022. In 2023, *The Consulting Report* named Dana Potthoff as one of the top twenty-five women leaders in consulting.

Dana often looks back on her move from California to New York City as her biggest confidence anchor. "They say if you can make it in New York, you can make it anywhere," she said. Today, she specializes in working with women, helping them to break belief barriers and shatter self-doubt.

STRATEGY FIVE: CULTIVATE CONFIDENCE

POWER STATEMENTS

Here are some affirmations to help you build unconditional confidence:

"I always communicate with confidence and unwavering truth."

"I'm worthy of great things."

"I build other people's self-esteem."

"I'm a leader who raises the confidence of the people on my team."

"I know that failure is temporary and setbacks will only make me stronger."

"I'm a capable, energetic person who has what it takes to succeed."

"I bounce back quickly."

"I always have the right perspective."

"My potential is sky-high; I'm confident I can succeed."

SPOTLIGHT ON STRATEGY FIVE:
KELLEY MCCLURKIN CULTIVATES CONFIDENCE

The vast majority of our coaching clients at Southwestern Coaching are directly involved in high-volume sales. They usually work in industries like insurance, banking, financial planning, or wholesale goods and services.

So when Kelley McClurkin heard about our coaching program, her first thought was that she didn't qualify. "I'm not a salesperson," she told us. Fortunately, our team at Southwestern Coaching had the opportunity to help her see how wrong she was about that.

Admittedly, it's easy to understand why Kelley didn't see herself as a candidate for coaching at first. She was the owner of a small business—Bread Kneads Bakery and Deli in Findlay, Ohio. She spent her days making pastries, quiches, specialty breads, and sandwiches for a niche clientele, relying mostly on foot traffic and word-of-mouth marketing.

She was also devoting a lot of time to being what we call a "firefighter." That describes how 99 percent of our coaching clients are operating on day one of the program: they first attack whatever is brightest and hottest at the moment, often neglecting what is

STRATEGY FIVE: CULTIVATE CONFIDENCE

"important" to deal with what seems "urgent." This strategy left her convinced she simply didn't have the time for anything else.

But Kelley wanted more out of her business, and she was wise enough to see that attracting wholesale customers was one powerful way to get it. That meant doing the one thing she had already said she wasn't capable of: becoming a salesperson. It also meant letting go of her mostly passive and reactive approach to running the bakery and replacing that with systems that were much more focused and intentional. Ultimately, she was more afraid of staying stuck than of leaving her comfort zone.

Over the years at Southwestern Coaching, we have refined the nuts and bolts of how to help a person—or a whole team—meet goals like Kelley's. Our modules help our clients with their visioning; time management; team recruitment, onboarding, training, and retention; performance metrics; culture-building; and so on. But Kelley's story illustrates the critical importance of one quality that only our clients can provide: they must possess the confidence that they have what it takes to succeed. Everything else depends on this.

Kelley's biggest obstacle was one she had erected herself when she said, "I'm a baker, not a businessperson." Happily, she proved to be highly coachable. One of our team members started coaching Kelley, and during the course of their work together, she:

- Gained control of her time with focused scheduling and clear boundaries.
- Moved beyond a "minimum wage" hiring mindset to build a team of motivated, like-minded people.
- Reverse-engineered her vision into tangible action items and then made them a daily priority.
- Overcame her fear of selling to people she didn't know and mastered the specific skills needed to do it well.
- Set the goal of landing eight new wholesale contracts—and then surpassed it by securing eleven very strong customers for her products.
- Sold her business in 2019 for far more money than she'd ever dreamed possible before coaching.

Along the way, every fresh win became a new confidence anchor for Kelley—another reason to believe in herself and her vision. Her initial negative self-talk ("I'm just a baker") gave way to a whole list of positive affirmations she used to guide her each day.

After selling Bread Kneads, Kelley set a new goal, one that would have terrified her before redefining possible in her life: she decided to find a job in sales.

[STRATEGY SIX]

Fortify Your Faith

"Faith is permitting ourselves to be seized by the things we do not see."
—Martin Luther, leading force in the Protestant Reformation

Like many of the strategies that will help you to redefine possible, faith can be difficult to describe or define because it's not always tangible. But I believe this strategy is one of the most important elements in achieving personal transformation. In fact, I would go as far as to say that true, meaningful change is possible only when you have faith.

One of the most powerful examples of faith I've experienced was during the week of September 11, 2001. I was wrapping up a successful summer in Greenwich, Connecticut, where I'd led a group of more than seventy West Coast college students who were selling educational products door-to-door in greater New York City. Greenwich, Connecticut, is a wealthy bedroom community located about thirty miles outside of the city. From Greenwich, it takes less than an hour to reach New York City by train or car, and in 2001, many households in Greenwich had someone who commuted there for work.

It was our last week in the program for Southwestern Advantage, and I was working fifteen-hour days to make six hundred deliveries that week. At 9:00 a.m. on Tuesday morning, I adjusted a stack of books in my arms and knocked on the door of a stately home.

A man answered the door, white-faced. "Have you heard?" he asked.

I shook my head. Wordlessly, he turned and motioned for me to follow him into the house.

The TV was blaring from the family room. Minutes before, he explained, American Airlines Flight 11 had crashed into the North Tower of the World Trade Center. "My wife works in the Twin Towers," he said. "She's there right now."

Shocked, I sat down with him to watch the live footage as smoke poured out of the top of the North Tower. Several minutes later, another plane, United Airlines Flight 175, hit the South Tower.

It was as if we were in a vacuum. Most of the phones in the area weren't working; the man couldn't call anyone, and he had no idea if his wife was alive. No one knew the casualties—the nightmare was playing out in real time. I stayed with the man until both towers collapsed. The books I'd brought were forgotten in a pile on the floor, an eerie reminder that everything was different now.

STRATEGY SIX: FORTIFY YOUR FAITH

As the week went on, I had to finish making my deliveries before I headed home. Everyone was gracious and understanding. I talked to hundreds of people and attended prayer meetings and candlelight vigils for missing and deceased Greenwich residents. With the number of banking professionals who lived the area, many people in Greenwich had lost a friend or family member. In all, thirty-two people from Greenwich lost their lives on September 11.

As they did for many people, the terrorist attacks gave me perspective. My previous few months had been spent traveling between my base in Greenwich and other hubs in and around New York City, and the noise, traffic, bickering, slander, and judgment had begun to wear on me. I had always believed that people were generally good, but at the end of that summer, I was feeling jaded about humanity. After 9/11, everything shifted, though. The community of Greenwich, located so close to Ground Zero, was no longer divided by sports teams, race, politics, or religion. People were united in their grief and eager to help one another. They looked each other in the eye and offered hugs to strangers. They made food for their neighbors and flew American flags from their cars and homes.

September 11 will always be one of the darkest times in our nation's history, but from where I stood, the country's collective response to it was overwhelmingly positive. There was beauty, unity, and national pride amid the suffering. In Greenwich, I rediscovered my faith in people.

FAITH: WHAT IS IT?

Faith is important to me, yet I struggled to write about it at first. Merriam-Webster defines faith as a "firm belief in something for which there is no proof; complete trust."[21]

But it's even more than that.

It's acting on an internal conviction. It is trusting in the unknown and the unseen and being willing to step out and act even though you don't know what is going to happen. Faith is that X factor, an intangible quality that makes all the difference when you have it. When you feel stuck or complacent, faith is the elixir. Best of all, faith is enduring. It doesn't fade.

Faith doesn't always have to be in a higher power. Just to be clear, you don't need to participate in a specific religion to have faith (although for some people—including me—that's a component). You can have faith in other people, in a company's vision, and in your calling.

As I mentioned, I have faith in the goodness of humanity, and I feel strongly that people can change. I have faith that dark, difficult circumstances can turn to light, as I saw happen during the terrorist attacks. I have faith that God will use everything that happens in my life for a purpose; I don't believe in coincidences.

The word *faith* is mentioned hundreds of times in the Bible, the best-selling book of all time.[22] In one of the most famous passages of the New Testament, the apostle Paul pairs faith with hope and love, stating, "Three things will last forever" (1 Corinthians 13:13). A lot of people put time and effort into love and hope. But rarely

STRATEGY SIX: FORTIFY YOUR FAITH

do people talk about how to have more faith. To redefine possible, though, you must have faith. Taking a leap of faith means moving past your doubts or lack of trust and acting on your convictions to start living the life you desire.

Faith works best when aligned with vision, whether that's going after a massive goal, starting a business, or taking a financial risk, such as hiring a coach, going back to school, or selling a house. Every world shaper throughout history has had an extraordinary amount of faith. Faith is necessary to accomplish big goals. We need to have faith to head into the unknown.

Without faith, we are more likely to give in to fear: We will hesitate to reach for big goals because we fear that we won't measure up. We will stay stuck because we worry that we won't be able to live up to people's expectations (or even our own).

Without faith, we cannot accomplish anything extraordinary. In August 1914, Sir Ernest Shackleton led a team of twenty-eight men on the Imperial Trans-Antarctic Expedition. Their grand objective was to reach Antarctica by ship and then cross the continent on foot, a feat no one had accomplished. Although Shackleton and his men failed to reach their objective, their journey became one of the greatest examples of endurance, resilience, leadership—and faith—in history.

Less than two months into the voyage, Shackleton's ship, the *Endurance*, became entrapped in pack ice on the Weddell Sea. The crew was forced to shelter in the moored ship for months as the ice drifted north. In October 1915, the pressure from the ice finally crushed the ship, and the *Endurance* began to sink.

The men salvaged as many supplies as possible and set up camp on a block of ice. Under Shackleton's faithful, steady leadership, the crew members lived on the ice floe for months, surviving by hunting seals and penguins. In April 1916, the ice cracked in half, and the group took a treacherous journey across the ocean in three lifeboats. They reached Elephant Island, an uninhabited, icy outcrop. Knowing they couldn't survive there for long, Shackleton decided he and a smaller group of men would sail eight hundred miles to South Georgia Island to seek help. Miraculously, they reached the island after sixteen days, but they landed on the uninhabited side. Shackleton then led two other men on a thirty-six-hour trek across the island's uncharted glaciers and mountain ranges. They reached a whaling station, where they finally organized a rescue mission. Remarkably, every single person from the *Endurance* survived.

Ernest Shackleton's story is an example of extreme faith. Shackleton had faith that he and his crew could undertake what many considered to be a heroic expedition in the age of Antarctic exploration. When the expedition ran off course, he had unflappable faith that his team could survive in one of the world's most hostile environments for almost two years. In turn, the crew had faith in their leader—believing that Shackleton had a plan, despite all the setbacks, that would bring them back alive.

FAITH VERSUS BELIEF

Faith is often confused with belief. Faith, however, is more abstract. It's about trusting that something will happen in the

STRATEGY SIX: FORTIFY YOUR FAITH

future. Faith can be difficult to describe, but you know when you have it or experience it.

Unlike faith, belief is more concrete, like having a set of principles. For example, when someone asks you about your beliefs, you might say, "I believe it's important to treat everyone with kindness and respect" or "I believe the most essential ingredient in a marriage is honesty." Beliefs are seen in the here and now, in the minutiae of your daily life.

If your beliefs are your map, then your faith is your compass. Everyone has faith. On a spiritual level, you have faith in what will happen after you die—whether you are a Christian who believes in heaven or an atheist who believes nothing exists beyond this world. On a business level, you have faith that you're going to achieve your goals, that your company will fulfill its mission, or that the economy will rebound. On a personal level, you have faith that your family and loved ones will be there for you in times of trouble.

When you have faith, you're focused on the future you have yet to see.

Gandhi had faith in his ability to create change in the world by organizing nonviolent protests. Alexander the Great had faith in his Macedonian army. Even the German philosopher Friedrich Nietzsche had to have faith in his reasoning to declare that "God is dead."

In the business world, there are many examples of people who have tremendous faith in their goals. The late Steve Jobs, who cofounded Apple, had faith in how people would act and what kind of lives they would want to live. He knew consumers would want to have the coolest phone or fastest, most interactive laptop. Everything he invented and invested in was about trends and people's emotions. When asked about what spurred him on through low points in his career, Jobs said, "It's not a faith in technology. It's faith in people."[23]

We all should have faith in people. Not everyone may be interested in technology, but everybody is invested in people, whether they're the head of a business, part of a team, or a member of a family. Of course, there's a caveat: if we put all of our faith and our hope in people, we will surely experience disappointment. That's why I strive to put my faith in God. Unlike people, God has never let me down.

HARNESS YOUR FAITH

Your sense of faith can be affected by the people around you. Motivational speaker Jim Rohn famously said that you are the sum total of the five people you spend the most time with. I agree. Do those five people have faith? If the people you surround yourself with are negative or they focus only on what won't work, then they are most likely minimizing your faith. But by spending time with people who have a strong and positive belief system, you can increase your own faith.

One practice is to develop a group of "advisors" or "board of directors" to consult for advice. Find two to five people who are aligned with your faith—whether it is your principles or spirituality—and ask them for advice on a regular basis. In seeking

STRATEGY SIX: FORTIFY YOUR FAITH

their wise counsel, you'll begin to let go of your pride and deepen your faith.

Your advisors may also be able to see problems that you can't. Having problems doesn't necessarily mean that you are making mistakes—only that you need to learn something from your experience. Your advisors will help you figure out the truth, and with their help, you will build a bigger, better, and more impactful life than you ever imagined.

You need input from real people who know you. Otherwise, you're just floating in whatever direction the wind is blowing. Your advisors—the people who are in alignment with where you want to be—can help you stay the course. They can encourage you to have faith so you don't waver or get off track every time things get difficult.

Reading books or listening to podcasts is another great way to harness your faith and get a new perspective on your current situation. To gain clarity and insight, you can create a habit of reading spiritual or sacred texts, self-help books, or biographies of people you admire. Or you might listen to podcasts or sermons that inspire you. When you listen to podcasts or read insightful books, ask yourself, "What is my destiny? What are my core beliefs? Why was I put on this earth?" Seeking guidance from wise people and accessing other resources will help you make short-term decisions that will guide the long-term trajectory of your life.

You may be reading this book because you're not sure what your destiny is or because you feel your life is at a crisis point. Maybe you've gotten discouraged about a situation where you used to have faith. Maybe you're wondering if you should keep pursuing a dream or if you should continue a business partnership that you once strongly believed in. Is it time to move on to something else, or should you have faith and keep walking along your current path? When you are at that critical juncture, how do you decide what to do next?

The answer is to spend more time praying, meditating, contemplating, and listening.

Listening is a skill that very few people have. And discernment is the muscle that comes from listening. Being able to discern what you're called to do or not do—and when you're called to start or stop—is a gift. Discernment allows you to determine whether you're making the right decision. Sometimes when you get focused and excited about something, you can make it happen because you naturally put in the effort—but that doesn't mean it's the right thing for you to do. When you don't allow events to unfold naturally, you are effectively forcing open a door. Ask yourself, "Am I kicking this door open, or is the door just opening before me so I can walk through it?"

If you feel like you have to kick a door open, then maybe that's a signal that you should pray, meditate, or listen before moving forward. But if the door is being opened before you, then that could be a sign that you should cross that threshold.

When you really contemplate, pray, and ask for things like clarity and discernment before you step out in faith, it's amazing how those prayers get answered. It's usually not at the time you hoped or in the way you expected—sometimes it's the complete

STRATEGY SIX: FORTIFY YOUR FAITH

opposite—but you end up getting exactly what you need.

When you align your faith with what you do every day, you will redefine possible.

HOLDING ON TO FAITH THROUGH HARD TIMES

Having faith is even more important when you experience hardship. When you face a challenge without giving up, you will strengthen your resolve and increase your faith too.

Everyone will face serious challenges sooner or later. If you are alive long enough, life will eventually punch you in the face. Like Mike Tyson said, "Everybody has a plan until they get hit."[24] When you do get hit, your faith—in people, in your mission, in God—will help you stand back up. Your faith will guide your responses and reactions to unexpected challenges and events that disrupt your life plans.

When you have faith, you can lean into the challenges ahead of you. You don't need to put on a smile and act like everything's rainbows and butterflies. Instead, you can embrace everything that's hard in life—the grit, the challenges, the news, and the stuff you fear.

Faith can grow with suffering. When you go through a challenge, you can struggle with it and wrestle with it, but don't say, "Forget it, I'm just going to give up." You must defy the quitter in you. Faith requires endurance. A lot of times, faith isn't rewarded quickly. But true faith is not shortsighted; instead, it helps you stick around for the long term.

I've talked a lot about my own crises, but I have also watched my colleagues use their faith to overcome many business challenges. In the first full year Southwestern Consulting was in business, the company earned more than $1 million in revenue. But years two and three were horrific. By 2008, it was over $1 million in debt. I was working directly for Southwestern Advantage at the time, and I remember when my friends, the cofounders of Southwestern Consulting, had to sit down with our CEO, Henry Bedford. Henry was blunt: "I don't know if a bomb needs to go off, but something drastic has to happen or this isn't going to work."

It would have been easy to give up, declare bankruptcy, and go find new jobs; after all, it was the middle of the Great Recession. But my colleagues had faith in the company's mission. They changed everything about Southwestern Consulting's business model and the way it operated, altering the compensation plan to be all performance-based and shutting down the seminar business. They started coaching, consulting, and speaking. They rode the roller coaster and stuck it out even though many people doubted them. And it paid off: just a few years later, the company had tripled in size.

Then the world shifted for everyone once again with the emergence of COVID-19. But unlike the Great Recession, this time the company was facing both a volatile economy *and* a global health crisis, the likes of which hadn't been seen in one hundred years. Fortunately, our leadership team had the tools—and faith—to address the crisis head-on. As I explained in the introduction, we used the RAFT technique to adapt to the times, and we recalled the lessons we learned in 2008.

STRATEGY SIX: FORTIFY YOUR FAITH

How did we turn the business around? Each time, we had faith in what we did, faith in the people we worked with, and faith in the mission we're on to help people reach their goals. Even though we had to change our business model again, our mission—and our faith in it—never wavered. Did we experience a lot of suffering during those uncertain periods? Yes. But it increased our faith in our mission, vision, and value even more. From 2019 to 2023, Southwestern Consulting increased its revenue by 36 percent.

You, too, can rely on your faith when you face trials. The next time you see a challenge coming your way, instead of running from it, try to welcome it as an opportunity to strengthen your faith.

My wife, Desireé, took a major leap of faith years ago that transformed her professional and personal life. Long before I met her, she had faced a heart-wrenching challenge with life-changing implications. When she was a young, single woman working a corporate job in Kirkland, Washington, Desireé discovered she was pregnant. Marrying the father was not an option, and Desireé knew she would have little help.

It caused her to question everything—especially her own beliefs and values. Could she raise the baby and provide financially? Would she choose to, even if the answer was yes? How would this baby change her life and her dreams for her future? She had always hoped to be a stay-at-home mom, but Desireé felt that possibility slipping away. Scared, alone, and confused, she gave birth to a beautiful baby girl and named her Hartley.

Of all the life changes this decision brought about, Desireé was least prepared for how reluctant she would be to part from

Hartley during working hours. The thought of leaving her daughter at daycare and enduring long absences seemed excruciating to her. She didn't know how she would do it, but Desireé was determined to find a way to stay home with her daughter.

Around that time, she started making fashionable headbands for Hartley. When more and more people began admiring them—and wanting to know where she'd bought them—an idea took shape. What if her dream of being a stay-at-home mom wasn't gone after all? Could she build a business that allowed her to make a living and spend time with her baby at home?

Desireé believed the answer was yes. She had faith in her skills and in her vision of wanting to stay home with Hartley. In a giant leap of faith, she quit her job and moved in with her sister. There, at the kitchen table, Desireé's business, Harts & Pearls, was born. It was a struggle that involved a lot of sacrifice, long hours, and hard work, but within a couple of years, she and Hartley moved into a place of their own. Most years since then, the company has seen double and even triple growth in sales. In fact, since 2012, Harts & Pearls has sold more than $2.5 million in accessories, has shipped to every state, and is in over 250 retail locations. After running the entire operation for the first few years, Desireé now employs a team of seamstresses and assistants as well as an army of people to help market her products online, offer them to wholesale distributors, and sell them at craft events around the country.

What sets Desireé apart from thousands of other people who remain stuck in fear and want? Faith, and the willingness to act on it.

STRATEGY SIX: FORTIFY YOUR FAITH

BECOME A FAITH BUILDER

Now that you've read this far, I want to encourage you to watch the world more carefully. It may sound weird, but notice the suffering around you. Pay close attention to the redemption stories. You'll see stories of people overcoming adversity. You'll hear about people renewing their strength. You'll learn about people who defied the odds because they clung tightly to their faith. These reports will reaffirm the truth that we as humans were meant to overcome obstacles. Every person on this Earth has had setbacks, but when you are a person of faith, you can have greater hope.

On the flip side, many people struggle with their faith when facing significant trials. For those who are grieving the death of a loved one, dealing with addiction, or trying to revive their once-successful small business, it's easy to question things. But that's where you can step in as a faith builder. It can be hard to know what to say to someone in crisis, but one thing you can do is acknowledge their faith. You might say, "Your faith has always been so strong, and I know it will sustain you during this time." Or, "I admire your calm and peaceful outlook. I know you'll be able to shine through this." Or, "I have always admired your ability to see the good and to be patient with your circumstances."

By doing so, you're speaking your own faith into other people who might urgently need it. When the people around you are fearful, rigid, or full of doubt, your words can give them a dose of hope, strength, and courage—helping them take the leap of faith that they need.

Of course, in order to encourage others with your faith, you first have to extend grace to yourself. Faith and grace are tied together. Grace is a tangible way to show faith. I've met so many people who are working hard to redefine possible for their lives, but when they reach this stage, they get stuck. They are ashamed of how they handled a conversation or a confrontation at home or work. They're holding grudges for wrongdoings that colleagues, friends, and family committed months and sometimes even years ago. They can't move past their past! They think they are punishing the people who hurt or sidelined them . . . but without realizing it, they're really hurting themselves.

Grudges are the opposite of grace. I've coached countless people on how to show themselves—and others—grace and how to find freedom in forgiveness as they redefine possible. Once they let go of their "right to be hurt," they begin to shine. They can share their faith with others. They can see things in people that those people don't see in themselves.

If you haven't experienced grace yourself, it's hard to give grace to others. And yet without grace, it's hard to have faith, because grace is the action of faith. What a gift!

This chapter completes another formula:

Belief + confidence = faith.

If you embody faith, you can walk confidently in your beliefs. But it's hard to walk in faith if you're not confident, and it's impossible to live a life of faith if you're not solid in your beliefs.

STRATEGY SIX: FORTIFY YOUR FAITH

When fear or uncertainty has a grip on you, faith will bring you freedom and success. If you stay open, grow your faith, surround yourself with the right people, and embrace hard lessons, you will find new horizons and opportunities beyond your wildest dreams.

POWER STATEMENTS

To strengthen your faith, incorporate some of these affirmations into your daily practice:

"I increase the belief, energy, and confidence of every person I meet."

"I empathize with others' struggles, pains, and regrets and help them embrace truth, forgiveness, mercy, and love."

"My mission is to help others reach their greatest potential every day."

"God gives me all strength, courage, and hope."

"I have faith in humanity and believe in the greater good."

"I am a person of faith."

"My faith helps me overcome all obstacles."

"I listen to God and trust His leading."

"I choose to live a life of faith, not fear."

STRATEGY SIX: FORTIFY YOUR FAITH

SPOTLIGHT ON STRATEGY SIX:
JOSH HUDSON LEARNS TO FORTIFY HIS FAITH

Occasionally, people come to Southwestern Consulting seeking help with issues not covered in business school. Because of the nature of their companies, they are struggling, not with time management or hiring practices or long-term vision. These leaders are troubled by a much more common human challenge.

Family.

It can be hard enough to maintain healthy day-to-day relationships among team members who have only their professional lives in common. But when a business is owned and operated by one or more members of a family, the obstacles to success can have roots reaching back decades.

On paper, Josh Hudson was a model of success. When he came to me for coaching help, he had an enviable income and shared a good life with his wife and two kids. Josh was the CEO of Hudson's Furniture, a company his father founded in 1981, the year Josh and his twin brother, Adam, were born. Josh had helped steer the company through an impressive financial turnaround after it nearly cratered during the Great Recession. In 2017, Hudson's Furniture was named Retailer of the Year by the Home Furnishings Association. Hudson's boasted eighteen outlets across central Florida and was approaching $100 million in annual sales.

Yet when we started our journey, Josh was not fulfilled. He was putting in long hours and dealing with a lot of conflict at work. He was not sleeping well. He was irritable and depressed. Even more, he was unsure that any of the unhealthy dynamics at work would ever change. Josh was unable to enjoy the fruits of his success because he was stuck in emotional and behavioral patterns with his brother, father, and others in the workplace. These interactions had tainted everything else about his daily experience of life.

"I know I was in danger of being less than my best for my wife and kids," Josh admitted. "And I had begun taking out my frustration on members of my team who had nothing to do with the real problem."

After several sessions and lots of listening to Josh's story, it was easy to see what lay at the core of his struggle: a lack of faith.

I'm not talking about spiritual beliefs but about another kind of conviction that keeps most people going in hard times. Josh was beginning to lose faith that his professional life would ever really improve. This desperation had only increased his impulse to exert

STRATEGY SIX: FORTIFY YOUR FAITH

control and to resist what he perceived as injustice. It was destroying him and harming all his relationships, professional and personal.

Over many months, we worked together to change how Josh saw himself, focusing on restoring his belief that he could take charge of his own experience and improve it. Rather than simply agreeing with Josh that his family dynamics were difficult, I helped him to accept his situation. He soon understood that his circumstances would only change when he had *faith in himself* and in his own ability to improve a very difficult family partnership. I helped Josh realize that after so many years of frustration, he could finally find peace in his work. His vision for himself and for his company would be truly possible if he had enough faith in himself and his ability to make changes.

To help him do that, I shared many tools for emotional self-management to help transform his reactive habits into healthy coping mechanisms. With a lot of hard work, Josh relaxed into a more peaceful and accepting version of himself and was able to develop his new faith: in himself, his company, and his future.

[THE PAYOFF]

Prepare for Impact

> *"So leave everything on the court. Leave the game better than when you found it. And when it comes time for you to leave, leave a legend."*
> —Kobe Bryant, basketball icon

Redefining possible isn't just about making a difference in your own life. The six strategies in this book—focus, ownership, vision, belief, confidence, and faith—are designed for you to transform yourself so that you can then reach out to help others.

It's important to note that impact itself is not a strategy. After all, leadership is not declared. You don't just get to decide one day that you're going to make a difference. Impact is the result, the payoff, the outgrowth of all the work you've done. True impact takes time.

As you read this chapter, I want you to think about how you can impact the people around you. One of the most powerful opportunities to make an impact is during times of crisis.

Challenges allow people to create impact by offering emotional support, showing up, and helping out in tangible ways, such as through meals, prayers, gift cards, and financial assistance.

I experienced that firsthand when Van was diagnosed with leukemia in 2016. As Desireé and I shepherded our son through doctors' appointments and treatments, I was crushed by a crippling sense of helplessness and failure. After all, I believed it was my job as Van's father to keep him safe and give him a happy, healthy life. Up against a mortal enemy, I felt utterly impotent and alone. Fortunately, I didn't feel that way for long. As the Beatles song says, I had "a little help from my friends." My friends reminded me that I am part of something larger than myself, which had a significant impact on my entire family.

My close friend and mentor John Dammarell, whom I introduced in chapter 4, spent hours with us when everything was turned upside down. He and his wife, Karilyn, dropped everything to come to Seattle Children's Hospital, which was located an hour from their house. In addition to sitting bedside, John followed up by scheduling regular times for him to visit. John knows what it is like to have a child in medical crisis, and he was the example I needed. He taught me how to be there for my family and sick son, and he showed us all incredible compassion and empathy. I'll always be thankful for the way that John generously poured into our family.

Dan Moore, another longtime mentor, also made an impact by pledging to come see us. That didn't mean a short car ride across town to our house. I live in Seattle, Washington, and I am the only senior partner at Southwestern Consulting working remotely. As the president of Southwestern Advantage at the time, Dan was working out of our headquarters in Nashville, Tennessee. Dan made good on his promise to visit. He took us to dinner, and his presence brought us peace and perspective during a time of so much adversity. His encouraging support meant the world to my entire family. He delivered a tangible message in person: no matter how far the distance, you are not alone.

Dan wasn't the only one from Southwestern who showed up during the crisis. Over the following months, we received invaluable help from the whole team at Southwestern Consulting. The company raised money to help with medical bills and lost income, and team members stepped up to assist with my clients and coaches so that I didn't have to worry about letting anyone down. It was peace of mind and borrowed strength that I desperately needed at the time. My tribe rallied around me and made it possible for me to fully be there for Van and my whole family.

The company's support had a ripple effect: it not only impacted our family but also made a difference in the lives of all our team members. By making an impact in one person's life, our whole team at Southwestern Consulting grew closer and became stronger for it.

Our friends' influence didn't end there. After Van was healthy, our team members and close friends inspired us to pay it forward. Since then, Desireé and I have been able to encourage many families whose children are facing cancer and other medical emergencies—transforming our family's trial into a story of impact and hope.

YOU WERE CREATED TO MAKE AN IMPACT

Once you have worked through the strategies to redefine possible, you'll discover that it's easy to make an impact. Your outlook changes. Everything in life becomes sweeter. Things aren't just good—they are great! Living a life in which you have redefined possible takes the mundane of your day-to-day existence and transforms it into a grander picture. You are thrilled to help others because you know the point of life is impact. I like to share the analogy that redefining possible is like driving down the road and suddenly hearing your favorite song come on your playlist. Your mood lifts, you start smiling and singing, and you stop worrying about getting to your destination in record time. You're in the right headspace, and you can't wait to share the strategies with others.

This doesn't mean that life is perfect. Your problems don't suddenly go away; you still have tough decisions to make. But you do have shorter valleys and higher peaks. Why? You don't let hard decisions or setbacks hold you back from fulfilling your vision. And you work to help others reach their highest peaks too.

True impact should feel like a calling. You must be willing to be selfless. Ask yourself: "Have I been put on this earth to help others? Am I here to lighten their load? Am I here to inspire them? Am I truly present? Do I believe in my purpose? Can I get people fired up about their own mission and goals?" If you answered yes to any of these questions, you're ready make an impact on those around you.

There is a term for the moment when you stop focusing on yourself, let go of your ego, and start putting others first. In the

Bible, the concept is loosely called "dying to yourself." (This concept can be seen in many passages in the New Testament, such as Galatians 2:20, Ephesians 4:22–24, and Philippians 3:8.) This idea is not exclusive to Christianity, though; most of the major world religions encourage selflessness.

It's much easier to just focus on getting accolades like trophies and recognition, because those are tangible measures of your success. Acknowledgment feels wonderful, but having something more solid, yet intangible, at the heart of your efforts and actions feels even better. And that something is the satisfaction that comes when you focus on serving others.

Dan Moore, who flew from Nashville to Seattle when I needed support, is one of the most selfless people I know. As the former president of Southwestern Advantage, he's impacted the lives of countless people. That's one of the reasons I asked him to write the foreword to this book!

I met Dan when I arrived at the company's Nashville headquarters as a college student in 1994. He quickly became a role model and close friend. I've spent time with Dan in many different social situations over the last thirty years. We've attended hundreds of dinners together and gone on numerous trips around the world. And in all that time, I don't recall ever hearing him talk about himself without first being asked.

Yes, you read that correctly: Dan Moore doesn't talk about himself. He doesn't monopolize conversations, tell long-winded stories about his life, or interrupt others to give his opinion. He doesn't try to one-up people or cut conversations short so he can go "work the room." Whether Dan is advising college students about their sales business or having a casual dinner with friends, he always focuses on other people. Dan asks open-ended questions and sincerely listens when others talk. He enjoys watching people interact. He makes everyone from strangers to close friends feel important, validated, and heard. And he doesn't do it for show—he can recall details from conversations he had months ago!

Several years ago, I felt inspired by Dan to take a long look in the mirror. I knew I was having too many conversations about myself. My coaching business was thriving, and I was spending more time than necessary talking about my "wins." I was excited about my progress at work and the mission we were on, but I realized I wasn't really listening to people as well as I could be. So, I decided to refocus on truly putting others first. I concentrated on being present and thoughtful, and I asked for accountability from my mentors and advisors. It took a lot of work, but now people tell me that listening and being authentic are two of my biggest strengths!

As Dan has shown me, sometimes you can make the biggest impact just by putting others first.

Being selfless is radical; in fact, it's countercultural. The truth is that most people are so focused on themselves that the only lens they can see through is their own selfish thoughts, desires, and outcomes. They spend a mind-boggling amount of time worrying about what other people think. They fixate on how they look, whether they sound smart or funny, and what other people say about them—so much so that it completely prevents them from living a life of impact.

Still not sure how to start to make an impact? As I've said before, you can begin by meditating, reading, praying, or simply paying attention to what inspires you. Maybe you want to try visualizing, thinking, and planning. Or you could go for a walk, get some fresh air, and turn off your phone. Either way, use that time to regain perspective. Quiet time will center you. If your head and heart aren't in the right place, you probably won't be able to make much of an impact.

Once you're ready, you will find many opportunities to influence the lives of those around you. By being authentic and vulnerable, and sharing your struggles and the mistakes you've made, you can help people when they're at a crossroads or dealing with difficulty. You can inspire people to keep striving, stay positive, and make the right decisions during difficult times. You can help people accept their circumstances so they can move forward. Another way is to be there for others when they need you the most, such as showing grace, love, and mercy to someone who has been condemned by society or abandoned by their friends. Finally, you can help in practical ways . . . just like John Dammarell, Dan Moore, and the Southwestern Consulting team did when they supported me after my son's leukemia diagnosis.

GET IN THE TRENCHES

One of the best ways you can impact your team at work is to get in the trenches with them. I believe that just as you lead by example, you create an impact by example too.

The first thing you must do is go through the fire yourself.

One of my mentors, Spencer Hays, used to say that you can't teach what you don't know and you can't lead where you won't go. If you want to be a leader, then you have to take on the challenge of doing all the hard parts of the job and mastering them first. You must be able to do what you're asking others to do, especially if it's something worthwhile, difficult, and impactful.

That's what it means to lead by example.

Look in the mirror and ask yourself, "Am I actually doing the things I'm asking other people to do?" If you're not doing those hard things, you will feel like—and may be perceived as—a hypocrite.

Impact starts with you.

At Southwestern Consulting, our coaches live and work remotely across the world. Because we believe so firmly in getting in the trenches as leaders, our team leaders spend time every year shadowing our team members. Whenever possible, we supplement our virtual efforts by going into the field. We see our team members' home office, we watch them do their jobs, and we coach them in person. To become a team leader, everyone must first qualify by personally selling a certain amount of business and coaching a specific number of years. They earn the right to lead other coaches *after* mastering the skills required first.

The global health crisis of 2020 required Southwestern Consulting to temporarily change the way we conducted our business. There were times we couldn't be with our team members in person, but we still worked face-to-face as much as possible, doing teleconference calls and virtual team bondings. We also got creative, ordering pizza to be delivered to each new coach's house so we could enjoy a meal together over video conference. Then, as soon as it was safe, we resumed our home visits and field trips.

Why do we make such an effort to be with our team? Because the impact of spending a single day together is worth a thousand emails or phone calls. I can't count the number of breakthroughs I've had by investing the time to get on an airplane and spend the day with someone. It's a memorable experience for me as well as the people I coach. The most authentic conversations happen face-to-face—when I show, as a team leader, that I am willing to see their world.

It also allows me to see things from my team members' perspective when I physically go into their office and house, meet their family, and see how they're organized. I see their computer and their desk, and I see the lens they're viewing the world through. I've literally gone to people's home offices and coached them to set up their office differently or to move their desk to a new area. I've said things like, "Hey, let's put your vision board up. Where's your script? Let's put your goals on the bulletin board."

Our company leaders know this without a doubt: showing up for our team members changes their life, it changes their trajectory, and it changes their perspective. By investing our time and showing up on our team members' turf whenever possible, we can help them see their vision clearly so they can focus on making an impact.

Maybe you can't easily hop on a plane. Or maybe you don't coach a team of people remotely—maybe you see your team members on a regular basis. Whether you work from home or work in the same building as your team, you can still make a huge impact simply by arranging to have lunch or coffee with a coworker or team member. It's hard to overestimate the importance of sitting down off-site and talking about things that matter.

Ask about their vision and purpose; find out why they're really here and why they are doing certain things. In fact, you should be having these discussions every time you talk to a coworker or one of your team members, either in person, on video chat, or by phone. Why is it so important? Because if you have a big enough vision, you can propel yourself through tedious or time-consuming tasks to make the change you desire—and you can inspire others to do the same. Albert E. N. Gray said in his classic 1940 speech to the life insurance industry that the most successful people create the habit of doing the things that unsuccessful people don't enjoy doing. In my coaching business, I have found this to be true. If you want to help people make an impact, start by teaching them that what they view as the daily grind is actually something they need to fall in love with doing in order to achieve their ultimate vision.

That shift in perspective will completely change their life.

Recently, I was explaining the relationship between impact and redefining possible to a teammate. It finally clicked for her when I described the opposite effect of not taking action, not having a vision, and not wanting to make an impact. "The opposite of impact," I explained to her, "is insignificance. It's having a full bank account but an empty soul. It's having focus, confidence, and drive but not using those qualities for good. All the accolades in the world won't bring love and connection. Impact is the way I want to live. It's the legacy I want to leave with my family."

WATCH FOR THE RIPPLE EFFECT

Many of us like solid results, and uncertainty frustrates us. Although we might be able to count thank-you cards and compliments, we find it hard to figure out how to measure impact.

When thinking about how to quantify the impact you're making, remember that it is complicated. You might make a modest impact just by having excellent principles and being a model of service. Or you may help one person who was ready to quit his or her business, marriage, or even life. That act can be worth as much as helping millions of people with smaller problems.

This ripple effect of impact on one client's life is exactly what I'm talking about—the individual touchpoints we can have in several areas of life.

Impact can be created in a variety of different ways. It might be as simple as taking the time to listen to someone in need. Or it might look like helping someone who isn't living by the right principles, is drifting, lacks a vision and mission for their life, or is just being reactive rather than proactive. Your impact will be evident when you help them find clarity, have a vision, or live by the right principles, ultimately changing their life in a positive way.

You create an impact when you lead by example, show others the right way to live, and help other people rather than focus on yourself. When you follow the strategies in this book, making them the basis for how you live your life, you change your lens.

Your focus becomes about what you give and how you help others.

I've been a leader in the workplace for many years, and I know this is true: when you are selflessly helping others, without an agenda, and have your heart in the right place, people will thank you and tell you that you've made an impact in their life. They'll tell you about their transformations.

It's a cycle. You help people, then they help other people, and then they help other people, multiplying the effect.

One person can have a tremendous impact. For example, take a single coach working at Southwestern Coaching, the one-on-one coaching business that is part of Southwestern Consulting. Southwestern Coaching works directly with more than one hundred coaches worldwide. Each coach has thirty clients on average, so that's over three thousand clients reached per year. Those clients are growing in life—in their financials, in how they use their time, and in their purpose—which impacts their family members, coworkers, friends, and neighbors. And that's just one coach living out his or her vision of helping others achieve their goals.

Several years ago, my son P. K. surprised me while I was driving him home after some one-on-one time. "Dad," he said nonchalantly, "you're not like my friends' dads." I asked him why he thought that, and his response floored me. "Well, you just seem to act differently than they do," he replied. "You're always talking about how much you love your job and you've shared stories of how people you work with live great lives. My friends' dads don't love their jobs. I'm glad you're my dad and that you're helping people."

I almost had to pull over to get the tears out of my eyes! There's no trophy in the world that would make me feel happier than hearing that my son could see the difference I was making in other people's lives. (More recently, he said he would love to do what I do when he's older. I couldn't be any more grateful to hear that!)

MAKE IMPACT YOUR LEGACY

As I've said, impact is mostly intangible.

I'm not Bill Gates or Warren Buffett, who can make a big impact because they can donate billions of dollars to various causes. But just because I can't give billions of dollars to charity doesn't mean I can't have just as much of an impact on the people I meet every day. In fact, impact has little to do with money or financial goals.

Perhaps the ultimate measuring stick for impact is how many people show up to your funeral. This occurred to me when attending the memorial service of one of my coaches, Mark Stacey, and seeing how much of an impact he made in the lives of thousands of people. I first discovered the extent of Mark's influence when I hired him in 2015 and was checking his references. I was blown away. Over and over, people said that Mark was the number-one person who had impacted their life. I soon realized what they meant. During the eight years that Mark worked with me, he was unfailingly kind. He spoke highly of everyone he knew. He treated every person he encountered like they mattered.

When Mark passed away in November 2022, I flew to Austin, Texas, for his celebration of life. Countless people—including family members, friends, coworkers, and coaching clients—also traveled from out of state. The room was filled with abundant joy as person after person got up to tell amazing stories about Mark and the influence he'd had on their life. I was privileged to be the last speaker, and I talked about the many times that I saw Mark put aside his own struggles to help other people. Mark was a successful businessman and coach, but his real treasure was the way he had reached so many people.

I believe that creating positive change in people's lives is literally the most rewarding thing you can do. Scientist, naturalist, and humanitarian Dr. Jane Goodall is often quoted as saying, "What you do makes a difference, and you have to decide what kind of difference you want to make."[25]

You and I may not become household names, but we can make an impact on our own household, which will in turn change our communities, workplaces, and beyond. In the end, if we can teach our children how to redefine possible for their lives, and they in turn teach it to their children, and so on, we will leave the greatest legacy and lineage we could ask for. I hope that, like Mark Stacey, at the end of my life, people will be lined up at my funeral to share stories of how I positively impacted them and others.

You now, at your fingertips, have the greatest formula to change your life. The strategies I've shared in this book are like ingredients for your favorite recipe, and your impact is the result. You'll need to follow the recipe order and make sure you didn't forget anything. It's a lot of hard work, but when you stay consistent and follow through, the yield will be incredibly fruitful.

THE PAYOFF: PREPARE FOR IMPACT

The unbridled joy you'll get after redefining possible, plus the peace you'll have in knowing that you've done all you can to transform your life, means that your life can have an effect that ripples throughout generations.

Your impact can be your legacy, helping you to redefine possible.

POWER STATEMENTS

As you get ready to redefine possible, focus on the idea of impact and the connections in this chapter. Here are some affirmations to keep these ideas at the top of your mind:

"I'm going to keep doing the right thing and focus on impact."

"Money comes and goes, but my impact on someone's life lasts forever."

"I positively impact every person I see."

"I use my time and resources to help others in any way I can."

"I help people reach their goals in life."

"My impact is my legacy."

"I'm the light for the people around me."

"I can change the world with small acts of kindness."

"My smile/ability to listen/hospitality/compassion creates an impact."

_____

_____

_____

_____

_____

_____

_____

_____

SPOTLIGHT ON IMPACT:
NOLAN PATTEE PREPARES FOR IMPACT

When Nolan Pattee heard about Southwestern Consulting, he was already a successful insurance agent and financial advisor running his own agency for Bankers Life and Casualty Company. He had a comfortable six-figure income and had grown his agency to a team of twenty people.

Nolan wanted more, though. When he signed up with Southwestern Consulting for one-on-one coaching, his business was not yet among the top one hundred agencies in the Bankers Life network, but he was determined to reach the top fifty. He also wanted to grow his personal income to $400,000 a year. It was what is commonly called a "big, hairy audacious goal."

One immediate obstacle he faced was the challenge of keeping tabs on offices in eight locations. Remote management is never easy, but Nolan seemed especially vulnerable to taking things personally when thorny issues arose. Those constant mental and emotional distractions threw off his ability to focus on what was important to the business as a whole.

In time, he would adopt the techniques his coach gave him for streamlining communications and accountability. Yet this would prove to be a relatively easy fix in comparison to the real challenge: Nolan's vision for himself and his company was entirely one-dimensional. For him, it was all about the money and winning.

That single-minded goal dominated Nolan's decisions—including how he went about recruiting, onboarding, training, and retaining team members. He looked only for people who shared his financial goals and assumed that, so long as everyone was making money, nothing else mattered.

He admitted to his coach that this attitude wasn't serving him very well when the coach pointed out the obvious: this prevented others from reaching their own goals. Something needed to change.

There is nothing wrong with seeking financial rewards. The problems arise when making money becomes the *only* reason for investing so much time and effort into a business. That's because, as much as we need it to survive, money will only make us so happy.[26] In fact, it is one of the flimsiest possible answers to defining a person's *why*. Many well-meaning people have learned that it often feels hollow and unfulfilling to reach purely financial goals; paradoxically, it can weaken a person's motivation to go on.

To help Nolan see this, his coach insisted he create

a vision board—a visual representation of what he wanted to achieve with his success. At first, Nolan was reluctant to commit the time and energy to create a proper vision board. But in the end, he relented—and it completely transformed his approach to business and life. He learned his previous vision had failed to include anything that would fit under the most important *why* of all: to make a positive impact on others.

Nolan quickly saw that what he really wanted was to be present in the lives of his kids, to take them on adventurous trips, and to make it to all their sports meets and games. He also wanted to build meaningful relationships with the people on his team. "I never really spent time with them before," he said. "Now I get to work with friends, not just employees."

His personal awakening was so transformative that he paid for everyone on his team to learn how to create their own vision board. Today he devotes a significant amount of time and resources to maintaining a company culture that values more than just money.

Not surprisingly, that hasn't stopped him from meeting his financial goals. Within five years of setting his first "audacious" goal, Nolan's agency was among the top ten in the company. His personal income topped $700,000, and his team grew from twenty people to more than eighty. Yet more important, he was able to realize his dream of buying a farm where he can take time off to spend with his wife and four children. Nolan and his family have also been able to travel the world, making family memories and creating a lifelong impact on his children. At the end of the day, Nolan has redefined possible for himself and his family and has impacted his team and those around him, leaving a legacy that will last forever.

[CONCLUSION]

Possible Doesn't Happen Alone

Close your eyes. Listen to your heart. It's time for you to redefine possible.

I'm excited to get to the end of this book. I have shared many ideas on how to redefine possible, and now I'd like to draw a few final connections between some of the concepts we have explored.

I have taken you on a journey from focus, ownership, and vision to belief, confidence, and faith—and then finally to impact. At the beginning of this journey, you might have had one definition of the word *possible*. But now that you've reached this stage and redefined possible for yourself, you can see that everything is possible, no matter what your circumstances are.

Once all the pieces come together, you will feel more serene and peaceful. By fully letting go of all the stress, clutter, and need for control, you will be able to just be present. Happiness is fleeting, but you will have joy that lasts. Rather than feeling pleasure momentarily and then falling into complacency, you will find a deeper sense of contentment.

True joy and peace are yours to have.

The first formula I shared with you involved the strategies in chapters 1 through 3—focus and ownership combine as vision. (Focus + ownership = vision.) In the second formula, covered in chapters 4 through 6, belief and confidence combine as faith. (Belief + confidence = faith.) When you take the end results—greater vision, deeper faith, and bigger impact (chapter 7)—you'll see that they allow you to reach your whole goal: redefining possible. When your vision, faith, and impact are strong, it changes everything.

You have a calling, which is your vision, to motivate you to follow through and master the details of what you hope to achieve. You have resilience, hope, and a heart to serve, which is faith at its strongest. And you have impact, which is drawing people to you and inspiring and guiding your team, family, friends, neighbors, and coworkers with the big and small things you do each day. You know that you can have all the money, devices, and trophies in the world, but those things won't give you one lick of joy if you're not making a true impact.

From there, nothing will hold you back.

This freedom is exhilarating. How many times have you been told "No" or "You can't go there" or "You can't do that"? Pretty much since the day you were born, right? After reading this book, you know better than to listen to limiting statements. Now you've learned to gain freedom by redefining what really is possible. Instead of feeling gripped by limits, you will feel the freedom that these strategies bring.

CONCLUSION: POSSIBLE DOESN'T HAPPEN ALONE

A famous advertising campaign featuring Muhammad Ali and other elite athletes once asserted, "Impossible is not a fact." I agree! What one person calls "impossible" is just his or her opinion. Impossible odds create potential, impossible situations are temporary, and impossible circumstances are only what you make them. In fact, like the ad famously stated, the word "*impossible* is not even a declaration."

Instead, "it's a dare."

YOUR DAILY WORK: THANK, ASK, SURRENDER

Redefining possible will require a commitment that you'll need to renew daily. Continuing to practice the strategies is like exercising or eating healthy—it's something you must do consistently to see results. Otherwise, if you don't keep up the work, you could easily slip back into your old ways.

The shape this work will take is up to you. For example, if you are someone who likes to meditate and center yourself in nature, you can take time to soak in the beauty and acknowledge the goodness you see and have in your life. If you are someone who prays, you can recite a daily prayer of gratitude for everything you have been given. As the stories I've shared in this book show, I believe that all the good things I have were given to me—and none of these gifts is something I deserve. So I should be over-the-top thankful for every blessing I have.

You'll also have to know how to ask for help. If you have enlisted the help of friends and mentors, you can ask for their advice. If you're going on a spiritual journey, you can say, "Hey, I can't do this without you, God." Beyond that, you need to know specifically what to ask for—whatever you're lacking. What are you looking for? Wisdom, discernment, confidence, powerful thoughts, the ability to have hard conversations?

Some of us need to consistently ask for forgiveness for pride and selfishness. No matter how good you get at this, your pride and selfishness may still be there, whether you like it or not. Ego is a dragon that you may have to slay every day. The enemy is the ego, and the battle is for your mind. Others might struggle with doubt or anxiety. If that's a challenge for you, then it's important for you to set those fears aside and pray for peace and strength.

Even as you get specific in asking for help, you must also realize this isn't something that you can "will" to happen. In fact—and this may be completely different from what you have read in other self-help books—if you think you can just "will" these changes into existence, that's a sign that you're in the danger zone. If you try to force things to happen, then you'll typically get the opposite of what you want because you're not doing the hard work to achieve it. You can't just decide one day to "positively think" your way into redefining possible.

Instead, take whatever it is you feel you need and want—whatever you're trying to will to happen—and submit it to God or to a higher power. Don't forget to hold those grains of sand loosely. As you submit spiritually, you are allowing for what's meant to be. When you do this, you are saying, "If this is supposed to happen, let the door open, and I'll walk through it. That'll be my sign. And if this is not supposed to happen, if this is not the

CONCLUSION: POSSIBLE DOESN'T HAPPEN ALONE

path that I should have in front of me, then I'm fine with that too. I'm fine with whatever direction I am being led. I'm going to be ready, I'm going to prepare myself, and I'm going to be open to the opportunity."

What you will be left with is a feeling of peace, a quiet certainty that cannot be found any other way. When you develop the qualities I've discussed—when you really have faith and the kind of confidence, personal vision, and impact we talk about—everything will be exactly as it should be.

REDEFINING POSSIBLE MAKES *ANYTHING* POSSIBLE

I don't want to leave you with the impression that I have this all figured out. I have made many mistakes and have had to course correct. I am not a perfect example to be held up. I simply have a vision for the future, and I work to redefine possible in my own life every single day.

I'm so grateful to work for a company whose mission is to change lives. Whenever Southwestern Coaching enrolls a new client, we call this enrollment a "life impacted" or a "life changed." My business goal is to help as many people as possible transform their lives. I often ask myself, "Can one person enroll more clients than anyone ever has in the history of the company? Can one person recruit and lead more effectively than anyone ever has in the company?" If I'm personally selling, recruiting, and leading, then I am reaching the trifecta—the three parts of Southwestern Coaching that we set as our standard.

But that's only one part of my life. In my personal life, I have other goals.

For example, I have challenged myself to reach a new fitness goal while still having my evenings and weekends to focus on my family and truly be present. I've involved my family in this aspiration, and I am allowing my spiritual life to guide me and be at the true center of it all. I'm getting to the point where I see what life looks like as I'm redefining possible in the present and the future, rather than focusing on what I've done in the past. I always tell groups in workshops I lead, "I'm no different than anyone in this room. I'm just trying to be a little better today than I was yesterday."

DON'T BE A LONE RANGER

As you can imagine, it's a lot of work to maintain all these attributes and feel motivated to redefine your boundaries. But you don't have to do this alone. We all need help.

I've talked about prayer and submitting to God or a higher power, but you can also seek help by hiring a coach. I firmly believe that everyone can grow from coaching, whether they're elite athletes or businesspeople.

We can all draw strength from each other. We can all find value in bouncing ideas off someone else, regaining perspective, and having someone help keep us accountable. I encourage you to find friends and mentors, even bosses, who are willing to give you honest feedback.

But finding someone who is dedicated to helping you become

CONCLUSION: POSSIBLE DOESN'T HAPPEN ALONE

your best self is the best gift. Working with a coach can put you on a fast track to accomplishing your goals. The right type of coach will customize a plan for you and your situation. Coaches are trained not to talk *at* you, but to listen *to* you. Coaches seek to understand what you're already doing well, identify where gaps exist, and confirm where you can use some support. And when you combine coaching with taking the steps to redefine possible, you'll have a really clear vision—short-term and long-term—of where you want to go.

If you are a longtime leader, executive, or mentor yourself, don't assume that coaching won't help you. In fact, you may need it more than anyone else, because you have the greatest opportunity to impact the most people. At Southwestern Coaching, we match our coaches to clients based on personality, and we can often accommodate requests about spirituality, gender, and in some cases, language. As this book goes to print, we have clients in forty different countries and over 170 certified coaches. Our coaches have reached more than twenty-two thousand individual clients, working with them one-on-one—ultimately increasing their clients' sales by over 25 percent.

If you want to explore working with one of our life-changing coaches, feel free to contact us at www.southwesterncoaching.com or www.redefiningpossible.com. In addition to offering personal, life-changing coaching, Southwestern Consulting provides a wealth of practical tips and information to its clients. I've included a small portion of this material in two appendices in the back of the book to help you in your journey to redefine possible.

THE HIGHEST CALLING

I wish you all the best. And I want to leave you with a message:

When you wake up every morning, renew your commitment to serving others instead of yourself. Challenges will come every day, fear will grip you, and shame and guilt will be a threat, but know that you can overcome your trials. Please live courageously and in peace, knowing that you can and will achieve your highest calling by serving others and lifting them up.

❦

Thank you for taking this journey with me. I think of you reading this book and opening your mind to my ideas . . . and I am grateful.

You've now got the strategies you need to redefine possible. There are no limits, not even the heavens! Embrace your soul, get ready for hard work, and then go live courageously.

The shattering of normal, the crushing of impossible, and the power of redefining possible begin now.

APPENDIX A

The RAFT™ Technique

Southwestern Consulting developed the RAFT technique to combat the tendency we all have to make excuses when things get hard in life.

As you redefine possible, you can use RAFT to encourage yourself to hold strong to your vision and your goals when life throws obstacles in your way. Be empowered to overcome all kinds of adversity with this technique!

A STRATEGY FOR DEALING WITH THE UNEXPECTED

Everyone has an excuse for why they cannot redefine possible and achieve their potential. I sure have had excuses as well.

Excuses come in different shapes and sizes. A lot of times your excuse for holding back is very real and difficult, such as the death of a loved one, a divorce, or a serious health challenge. Other excuses, however, may be less significant. These can simply be due to a lack of self-confidence or caused by uncontrollable external circumstances like the economy, the weather, the region you live in, industry regulations, or your family situation.

One of my mentors, the late billionaire Spencer Hays, always said, "There are two types of people in this world: one finds an excuse, the other finds a way. It doesn't take guts, gumption, or determination to find an excuse. Anybody can locate one. It takes quality people to find a way over, under, around, or right through any obstacle that stands in their way."

You may be worried that you are going to be left paralyzed by the pain that comes with change. But I'm not going to leave you behind—I'm going to offer you a life raft.

RAFT is a technique you can use to get unstuck when you are overwhelmed by life's challenging circumstances. This technique can help with adversity of all kinds, big and small. When you remember to apply the RAFT technique, you will empower yourself to overcome obstacles quickly and never make an excuse again. Let's look at the breakdown of the acronym RAFT:

APPENDIX A: THE RAFT TECHNIQUE

R: Realize an event is happening to you.

This first step is incredibly important: awareness. You must be aware that a difficult event is occurring, rather than ignore the situation or your feelings about it. It may sound strange, but many people I meet become so caught up in the day-to-day grind or get so myopic about their plans that they don't pay attention to what is happening right in front of them.

An example of this might be if your company hires a new sales director who decides to double your sales quota and implement a time-consuming reporting procedure. If you are like many people, you might rely on your past performance, believing that it will be good enough to do things the old way. But when your new boss gives you a negative performance evaluation or even a pink slip a few months later, you'll be forced to face your circumstances.

You'll know an event is happening to you when you notice that you are slowing down in your progress or making excuses about your lack of achievement. This affects your plan, pushing your goals "off schedule." That is your event. Events can be big (like getting laid off when you're the primary breadwinner) or small (like having your car break down or not passing a certification exam).

Once you realize something is getting you off schedule and you've identified your event, you are ready for the next step: acceptance.

A: Accept that the event is occurring.

It can be challenging to accept reality. Most people naturally resist accepting events that happen to them, especially if the situation feels extreme and unfair. As I often say, "It is my resistance to 'what is' that causes my suffering in life."

It can be difficult to accept when trials happen to you, because typically the event makes for a great excuse. It's easier to tell people that you have a new boss who is "out to get you" than to accept that you need to make significant changes to keep your job. After all, everyone loves a good dramatic story, and often when you tell other people about it, everyone around you will agree with how horrible your situation is. Then they might encourage you to relax, quit your job, ignore the situation, or do whatever is necessary to avoid the pain.

You can try to fight the situation at work by making excuses and playing the victim. You can ignore your problems at home by staying busy or numbing your pain with things like food, drinking, shopping, or exercise. You can even pay thousands of dollars and spend months in therapy. But no matter how you choose to handle the crisis, you eventually must come to terms with your situation and accept that the event happened to you.

F: Focus on what you can control.

The good news is that matter how bad or overwhelming your situation is, there are always three things in life that you can control: your attitude, your schedule, and your activity or actions.

Your attitude is a choice. You choose your attitude every day when you wake up in the morning. If you're in a bad mood—congratulations, it's your fault! If you're in a good mood—congratulations, that's your doing too! Throughout history, people have told stories

APPENDIX A: THE RAFT TECHNIQUE

about being in horrible situations—even being in concentration camps or sentenced to death—but they still found joy in something each day. It is possible to choose joy.

Your schedule is a choice. You determine what time you wake up and when you go to bed. You control your schedule and your time—and even how people communicate with you. You have the same number of minutes available today as anyone else. Playing the "I don't have time" game is self-sabotage. Again, if you don't like how your schedule looks—congratulations! It's your fault.

Your activity (or action) is a choice. Deciding *not* to do something is also a choice. For example, if you have a tough new boss, you can choose to focus on learning the new reporting procedures and maximizing your sales output, or you can put in minimal effort and vent to your coworkers instead. Either way, you control the activities you decide to take on every day: how many calls you make, your lack (or excess) of social time, and what you do or don't read, watch, and listen to. You also control things like whether or not you make it to the gym or cook a healthy dinner instead of grabbing fast food. You can decide how much time you want to spend on each of these different tasks. Your schedule is within your control—from the moment you wake up until you close your eyes to go to sleep at night. You set the boundaries around your time.

When you take responsibility, focus on what you can control, and stop making excuses about events that happen to you, you can begin to create your own normal and redefine possible.

T: Transform the negative event into positive momentum.
Let's revisit the example of having a new sales director. When you follow the RAFT technique—realize things are changing at work, accept that you have a new boss who has much higher expectations than your last one, and focus on what you can control (your attitude, schedule, and actions)—you will transform your situation! By not making excuses, you'll either boost your sales performance by learning some new strategies and systems or decide you need to go in a different direction and look for a better job where you can thrive.

I love sports because they provide countless inspiring stories of athletes who have successfully used these principles. For instance, what do Michael Jordan, Serena Williams, and Brett Favre have in common? Besides the fact that they're each one of the all-time best players in their respective sports, they all transformed negative events into positive momentum.

Brett Favre played one of the best football games of his life the day after his dad died. Michael Jordan was suffering from extreme flu-like symptoms in game 5 of the 1997 NBA Finals, but he still performed one of his most significant games ever. He led his team in the win over the Utah Jazz to take the series 3–2. Serena Williams suffered a life-threatening pulmonary embolism in 2011, forcing her off the tennis courts for nearly a year. She came back from her health crisis by winning her fifth singles title at Wimbledon and earning a gold medal in the singles event at the 2012 London Summer Olympics.

APPENDIX A: THE RAFT TECHNIQUE

GROWTH AFTER TRAUMA

One of the reasons the RAFT technique is so helpful is that it embraces a concept called post-traumatic growth. Sometimes events are straightforward, but oftentimes events can be traumatic. Experiencing personal growth after trauma, like joining a grief group after losing a loved one, can completely change your life. When you harness your emotions from a negative event and transform them to create positive momentum, you can break through to a whole new level that wouldn't have been possible otherwise. What was once a negative event can become a powerful tool for growth. An incredible transformation will take place when you embrace adversity and use it as fuel to perform.

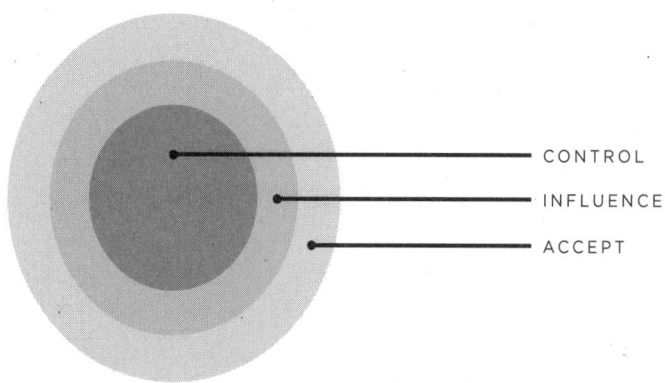

Realizing these traumatic events happened to you, accepting them, focusing on what you can control, and transforming the traumatic event into positive momentum can be exactly what you need to redefine possible and take your life to the next level.

© Southwestern Coaching, a division of Southwestern Consulting

APPENDIX B

Gratitude

Gratitude is not a specific strategy I have in the main text of the book, but it is a very important element in the journey to redefining possible.

I have spent countless hours working with my coaching clients on having an attitude of gratitude. Gratitude is something I also work on every day. It's easy to get caught up in waiting for something better to come along and stressing about "what if," but slowing down and reflecting on what you do have can help bring clarity to your vision and your goal to impact others as you redefine possible.

Gratitude takes redefining possible to the next level. In this appendix, I share some additional tips on gratitude and include a space for you to write out things you appreciate.

GRATEFULNESS

Being grateful is different from having a positive attitude. Having an optimistic outlook doesn't necessarily mean you are grateful for your current situation. As soon as you get in the mindset that you "deserve" things, you are in the trap of believing you don't have enough. Anything good is a gift. It's impossible to feel grateful if you feel entitled.

It's important to remember that you're on this earth to serve people. Looking for people you can serve every day will help remind you to live out an attitude of gratitude.

Keeping a daily gratitude journal can help keep you on track. Do you have a truck that runs or a friend who always picks up when you call? Maybe you have a dog that likes to cuddle, a low-interest mortgage, or a view of the mountains. Whatever the blessing is, write it down. When you're in neutral, it is easy to slip into a negative mood or attitude. If you remind yourself every day what you have to be thankful for, it will create a consistent attitude of gratitude.

COMPARISON IS THE THIEF OF JOY

Comparison causes stress and frustration and ultimately limits people's beliefs in what they think is possible.

It takes an extreme amount of self-control and mental toughness not to compare yourself to other people. Think about it. When was the last time you had any of the following thoughts?

- "I would be doing much better if I had Erin's territory."
- "I'm doing more work than Zach, and he needs to pick up the pace."

APPENDIX B: GRATITUDE

- "The only reason Anthony is successful is that he gets special treatment from the boss."
- "It's not fair that Lexy is getting paid as much as she is. I work just as hard, if not harder, than her."
- "Julio's marriage seems so much happier than my marriage."

The hardest part of not comparing yourself to other people is the fact that we, as humans, are hardwired to desire what we don't have. Have you ever seen a toddler walk up to another child and just take the toy they have? Being content with your current situation can be a challenge.

While it's good to be driven and to want to win, being too competitive with other people can end up being destructive. It's okay if your goal is to be number one because you think being number one is your potential. It's not okay if your goal is to be number one because you cannot stand the person who's currently number one and you just want to beat them. When people are too competitive with others, they tend to be territorial, selfish, and frustrated that they can't control what other people are doing.

We are called to live up to the potential that we have been given. Our ambitions should come from being motivated to do our dead level best every day. If your goal is to beat your personal best performance every day, then there will be no limit to what you can do!

Having gratitude can help you avoid comparing yourself to other people. It can also help you be content with what you have and break your own belief barriers of what you think is possible.

I often share this poem with our coaching clients, because it powerfully describes the importance of gratitude.

A Beginning of a New Day
This is the beginning of a new day.
God has given me this day to use as I will.

I can waste it or use it for good.
What I do today is important, because
I'm exchanging a day of my life for it.

When tomorrow comes, this day will be gone forever,
leaving something I have traded for it.

I want it to be gain, not loss;
good, not evil; success, not failure;
in order that I shall not regret the price I paid for it.
—Heartsill Wilson

(Legendary football coach Paul "Bear" Bryant famously carried this prayer with him in his wallet.)

CREATE A GRATITUDE LIST

On the following page, make a list of twenty things that you love about your life. Looking at this list every day will reinforce your attitude of gratitude as you redefine possible for your life.

GRATITUDE LIST: 20 THINGS I LOVE ABOUT MY LIFE

1. _____
2. _____
3. _____
4. _____
5. _____
6. _____
7. _____
8. _____
9. _____
10. _____
11. _____
12. _____
13. _____
14. _____
15. _____
16. _____
17. _____
18. _____
19. _____
20. _____

© Southwestern Coaching, a division of Southwestern Consulting

APPENDIX C

The Power of Self-Talk

At the end of each chapter, I shared power statements—positive affirmations for you to say out loud or write out and post where you can see them daily.

Seeing and saying positive affirmations can change the wiring in our brains to think more positively. This is the power of self-talk. In this appendix, I've included even more great techniques for developing your self-talk. It is one of the best things you can do to help achieve your goals.

WHY DOES SELF-TALK MATTER?

There is a great book on self-talk by Shad Helmstetter titled *What to Say When You Talk to Your Self*. The book includes five major principles to help improve our self-talk. It says:

- Success results from our actions.
- Actions are filtered by our feelings.
- Feelings are based on our attitudes.
- Attitudes come from our beliefs.
- Beliefs are purely programming.

SELF-CONFIDENCE CYCLE

We are being programmed every day whether we like it or not. We are programmed by the media, other people, and outside influences. Whether you choose to let yourself be programmed by society or choose to program yourself by using positive self-talk, the decision is yours.

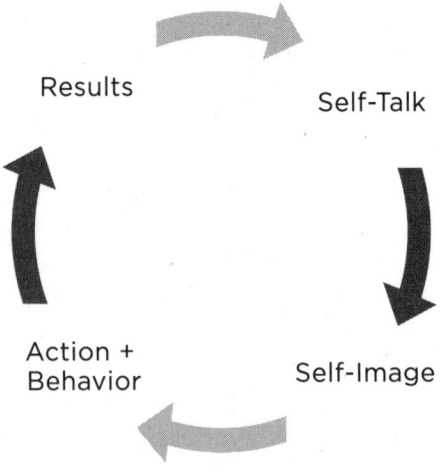

APPENDIX C: THE POWER OF SELF-TALK

POSITIVE SELF-TALK: THE POWER OF POSITIVE AFFIRMATIONS

> *"Self-talk is defined as what you say about yourself to yourself, and what you allow others to say about you, that you believe."*
> —Dan Moore

There is a misconception that self-talk is all about being positive. Self-talk has nothing to do with being a positive person. It has everything to do with looking in the mirror and honestly saying what you think about yourself.

Your self-talk is perhaps the most important thing in your life. The core of your self-talk is your belief system. Your beliefs construct your attitudes. Your attitudes determine your actions. Your actions come from your feelings. Your feelings come from your self-talk.

Below are some examples of affirmations that specifically relate to confidence.

- *Independence:* "I never have to be told what to do."
- *Execution:* "I actually do what I already know."
- *Studious:* "I am always eager to learn and never feel like I have arrived."
- *Coachable:* "I always work efficiently and follow the system."
- *Accountable:* "I never make excuses!" (e.g., I would have, but . . .)

- *Implement:* "I always use the notes I take."
- *Disciplined:* "I am always aware of the importance of my schedule."
- *Loyal:* "I support my teammates at whatever cost."
- *Objective:* "I remember to criticize or give feedback on the action and not the person, in private and not in public."
- *Determined:* "I can, I will, I'm going to . . ."

If someone stuck a recorder inside your brain over the past twenty-four hours, you would probably agree that the things you say to yourself would be scary. Most people spend their entire lives telling themselves what they can and cannot do.

> "The key to success is having amazing self-talk."
> —Spencer Hays

Your self-image is directly tied to your self-talk. When you look in the mirror, do you see someone who is unfit, ugly, dumb, a failure, a bad husband/wife, a lousy father/mother, a victim, a martyr, a jerk, a nag, a mediocre worker . . . or do you see someone who is fit, sexy, smart, a winner, the world's best husband/wife and father/mother—someone who will go over, under, around, or straight through any obstacle in their way? As humans, we are programmed to think a certain way, whether we like it or not. Either you choose to give up control of your own programming and let the media, society, or your friends and family program you with what you believe about yourself and the world, or you take control of your self-talk and start programming yourself with the things you want to believe about yourself and the world.

HOW TO WRITE GREAT AFFIRMATIONS

A simple way to change your life is to take what was previously a weakness or growth area and write an affirmation about it.

A great affirmation includes the following elements:
- First person [I]
- Present tense [I AM] or [I AM BECOMING]
- Powerful words that convey pictures or emotions

EXAMPLES OF POSITIVE AFFIRMATIONS

- "I am an unstoppable force!"
- "I can, I will, I am going to overcome any obstacle in my way."
- "Every no gets me closer to a yes."
- "I'm getting more organized every day."
- "If I see more, I sell more."
- "It's like me to hit my goals."
- "I finish strong because I work the numbers."
- "I like pressure; it brings out the best in me."
- "If it's going to be, it's up to me."
- "Calm and cool, I always deliver."
- "Fearless on the phone, 90 minutes of no distractions."
- "Every hour gets my best; every person gets my best."

If you want to take control of your self-talk, the most impactful exercise you can possibly do is to take out a piece of paper and write out a minimum of fifteen positive affirmations. Then, make ten copies of your affirmations and carry them with you, post them on your walls, share them with other people, and, most importantly, say them to yourself out loud every day.

APPENDIX D

Strategy Tactics

Throughout the book, I mention quite a few tactics and activities that you can pursue as you head down the road to redefining possible. I want to share them with you here, in one place, to help you achieve all you want in life.

These tactics provide practical ways for you to bring the strategies in this book to life. It's important to take the proper time to work through these prompts as you start to redefine possible.

THE TRUE-YOU INTERVIEW
Strategy Two—Ownership

Taking accountability is making the commitment to improve. This means being open-minded to feedback, especially in areas where you have weaknesses. However, when it comes to ourselves, we have blind spots because we can't see ourselves the way the people closest to us do. We can hold ourselves accountable to improving by asking others what they see in us.

The True-You Interview is a system for getting honest feedback. Through asking a series of seven questions to the people who know you best, you can learn about areas in which you might be excelling and other areas where there might be room for improvement.

Pick three to five people in your life you're fairly close with who would be honest about your strengths and your weaknesses. It could be a significant other, a parent, a best friend, or a coworker. The key is to interview people who will be totally honest and forthright. You can help by creating a safe environment for them. Tell them that whether it's good or bad, you want to hear it because you're focused on growth and accountability.

APPENDIX D: STRATEGY TACTICS

THE TRUE-YOU INTERVIEW QUESTIONS

1. What are my strengths?
2. What do you see as my strengths in my everyday life and business?
3. What are my weaknesses?
4. What doesn't work about the person I am?
5. What do other people count on me for?
6. What do other people know I can't be counted on for?
7. Is there anybody I should apologize to for wrongdoing?

Being truly accountable means that you must be vulnerable and totally open to feedback, both positive and negative.

In the space below, list three to five people who are close to you and would give you open and honest feedback to the questions above.

1. _____
2. _____
3. _____
4. _____
5. _____

VISION: YOU ARE IN CONTROL
Strategy Three—Vision

As you thought about your vision in chapter 3 and what you would like to be, do, and have in your life, you probably noticed how the world prescribes one way of achieving your goals. The journey to redefining possible is counterintuitive, though.

Most people think that life works like this. . . .

For example:
"If I had more money, then I could do the things I want and I could be happy."

Successful people understand that life actually works just the opposite. . . .

For example:
"I can be happy, which makes it easy to do the things required so that I can have more money."

APPENDIX D: STRATEGY TACTICS

20 "WHATS" TO FIND YOUR "WHY"
Strategy Three—Vision

1. What amount of money do you want to make?
2. What places would you like to visit in the world?
3. What type of job would you like to do each day?
4. What would your perfect day look like in terms of how you spent your time and what you were doing?
5. What are the characteristics of your perfect relationship?
6. What do you want to look like?
7. What do you want to give back to the world?
8. What do you want to be known for?
9. What are the things you believe in most?
10. What people can help you get to where you want to go?
11. What are the things you would like to have?
12. What are the most exciting things you'd like to try?
13. What events would you like to go to?
14. What type of house do you want to have?
15. What people would you like to meet?
16. What amount of money do you want to have at retirement?
17. What would you do if you knew you couldn't fail?
18. What things would have to happen in order to accomplish that huge dream?
19. What do you want people to think of when they think of you?
20. Who do you want to spend most of your time with?

15 GOALS TO ACCOMPLISH IN THE NEXT YEAR
Strategy One—Focus

In chapter 1, I discussed the power of writing out your goals on paper. I believe you can accomplish whatever you set out to do! Write out fifteen goals for the year below.

1. _____
2. _____
3. _____
4. _____
5. _____
6. _____
7. _____
8. _____
9. _____
10. _____
11. _____
12. _____
13. _____
14. _____
15. _____

APPENDIX D: STRATEGY TACTICS

IDENTIFY, DUPLICATE, PERFECT
Strategy Five—Confidence

In chapter 5, I discussed how to gain unconditional confidence as quickly as you can in order to redefine possible. To improve and increase your confidence, you can use the Identify, Duplicate, Perfect (IDP) technique, created by Southwestern Consulting's Dave Brown, to master your strengths.

It's easy to rely on others to give you feedback about what you should be doing better and what you already do well. However, you also have the ability to self-evaluate and determine these traits for yourself. No one knows you better than you do.

1. **Identify** the best version of you. What makes you great? At the end of a great week, look back and determine what you did really well. No matter how badly you think you did, there will always be a few things that you did right. It can be anything from how you greeted people to how you asked for referrals. What are your strengths? Think of three to four things you already know you do well.

2. **Duplicate** those things you already do well. Come up with a strategy to duplicate each one of those three or four things in every single presentation or project that you do. This allows you to master your optimal habits. Duplicate the version of yourself that you bring to the table when you're at the top of your game. Focusing on the strengths you already have helps you build confidence and gives you a positive anchor to rely on in any situation.

3. **Perfect** your strengths by planning to practice them. Look at your schedule and decide when you can put your strengths to use. Proactively planning when to use your strengths will give you confidence in each of those situations.

Focusing on what you do well will provide an anchor of confidence that grounds you. For example, going into a client meeting with the knowledge of what your strengths are can give you the confidence you need to take your skills to the next level. Incorporate the IDP technique into your schedule next week and notice the difference in your level of confidence.

Identify: _____

_____

_____

_____

Duplicate: _____

_____

_____

_____

Perfect: _____

_____

_____

_____

APPENDIX D: STRATEGY TACTICS

LITTLE VICTORIES
Strategy Five—Confidence

If you complete these ten "little victories" every day, you will have so much positive momentum that your confidence will be at a peak before you even start your workday.

1. Wake up, jump out of bed, and say, "It's going to be a great day!"
2. Hustle to the bathroom, look yourself in the eyes, and say a positive affirmation.
3. Do some kind of physical activity. Work out or do push-ups and sit-ups. Every day, try to do one more repetition than the day before.
4. While getting ready, say ten times, "I can, I will, I'm going to . . . [insert goal for that day]."
5. During breakfast, read something inspirational.
6. After breakfast, take ten minutes to review your must-dos for the day and visualize success in all of your activities.
7. On your drive to the office, listen to a motivational podcast or audiobook.
8. When you get to work, say something uplifting to the first person you see.
9. Say a positive affirmation out loud before your first phone call, meeting, or presentation.
10. Have your schedule ready and in front of you and strive to be on time for each event of the day.

© Southwestern Coaching, a division of Southwestern Consulting

Acknowledgments

Mom and Dad, you have believed in me through it all—including every boneheaded choice I've ever made. You've always been a shining example for me of God's love and grace. Thank you both. Desireé, you are like no one I've ever met, and I hope this book and I make you proud. I love doing life with you! You are truly my best friend. VPKH, my crazy kids, you make me whole. You three are the biggest reasons behind most of what I do. To my Southwestern family, I have found home, and I am grateful.

Endnotes

1. Charles Q. Choi, "Human Brain May Be Even More Powerful Computer than Thought," NBC News, October 30, 2013, https://www.nbcnews.com/sciencemain/human-brain-may-be-even-more-powerful-computer-thought-8C11497831.
2. Larry Alton, "Why Clutter Is Killing Your Focus (and How to Fix It)," NBC News, June 22, 2017, https://www.nbcnews.com/better/health/why-clutter-killing-your-focus-how-fix-it-ncna775531.
3. Tarek Amer, Karen L. Campbell, and Lynn Hasher, "Cognitive Control as a Double-Edged Sword," *Trends in Cognitive Sciences* 20, no. 12 (December 2016): 905–915, https://pubmed.ncbi.nlm.nih.gov/27863886/.
4. Catherine A. Roster, Joseph A. Ferrari, and M. Peter Jurkat, "The Dark Side of Home: Assessing Possession 'Clutter' on Subjective Well-Being," *Journal of Environmental Psychology* 46 (June 2016): 32-41, https://doi.org/10.1016/j.jenvp.2016.03.003.
5. Dr. Henry Cloud and Dr. John Townsend, *Boundaries: When to Say Yes, How to Say No to Take Control of Your Life*, rev. ed. (Grand Rapids, MI: Zondervan, 2017).
6. Ron Breazeale, "Thoughts, Neurotransmitters, Body-Mind Connection," *Psychology Today*, July 17, 2012, https://www.psychologytoday.com/us/blog/in-the-face-adversity/201207/thoughts-neurotransmitters-body-mind-connection.
7. *Merriam-Webster.com Dictionary*, s.v. "rationalization," accessed February 14, 2020, https://www.merriam-webster.com/dictionary/rationalization.
8. Malcolm Gladwell, *David and Goliath: Underdogs, Misfits, and the Art of Battling Giants* (New York: Little, Brown and Company, 2013).
9. Christopher N. Cascio et al., "Self-Affirmation Activates Brain Systems Associated with Self-Related Processing and Reward and Is Reinforced by Future Orientation," *Social Cognitive and Affective Neuroscience* 11, no. 4 (November 2015): 621–29, https://doi.org/10.1093/scan/nsv136.
10. Leena Guptha, "To Affirm or Not Affirm?" *Psychology Today*, April 25, 2017,

ENDNOTES

     https://www.psychologytoday.com/us/blog/embodied-wellness/201704/affirm-or-not-affirm.

11. Mayo Clinic Staff, "Change Your Mind to Grow," Mayo Clinic, November 5, 2021, https://mcpress.mayoclinic.org/healthy-brain/change-your-mind-to-grow/#:~:text=Adjusting%20to%20a%20growth%20mindset,learn%20and%20grow%20from%20them.

12. Nelson Mandela Foundation, "Biography of Nelson Mandela," Nelsonmandela.org, accessed April 7, 2020, https://www.nelsonmandela.org/content/page/biography.

13. Eilene Zimmerman, "Survey Shows Visualizing Success Works," *Forbes*, January 27, 2016, https://www.forbes.com/sites/eilenezimmerman/2016/01/27/survey-shows-visualizing-success-works/#7a7adc65760b.

14. Lien B. Pham and Shelley E. Taylor, "From Thought to Action: Effects of Process-Versus Outcome-Based Mental Simulations on Performance," *Personality and Social Psychology Bulletin* 25, no. 2 (February 1999): 250–60, https://doi.org/10.1177/0146167299025002010.

15. Jim Lohr, "Can Visualizing Your Body Doing Something Help You Learn to Do It Better?" *Scientific American*, May 1, 2015, https://www.scientificamerican.com/article/can-visualizing-your-body-doing-something-help-you-learn-to-do-it-better/.

16. *The Last Samurai*, directed by Edward Zwick, written by John Logan, featuring Ken Watanabe and Tom Cruise (Los Angeles: Warner Bros., 2003), DVD.

17. *Merriam-Webster.com Dictionary*, s.v. "*confidence*," accessed February 14, 2020, https://www.merriam-webster.com/dictionary/confidence.

18. Ziglar Inc., "Your Altitude," Ziglar.com, accessed April 17, 2020, https://www.ziglar.com/quotes/your-attitude-not-your-aptitude/.

19. Cloud and Townsend, *Boundaries*.

20. National Institutes of Health, "Breaking Bad Habits: Why It's So Hard to Change," *NIH News in Health*, January 2012, https://newsinhealth.nih.gov/2012/01/breaking-bad-habits.

21. *Merriam-Webster.com Dictionary*, s.v. "*faith*," accessed February 14, 2020, https://www.merriam-webster.com/dictionary/faith.

22. Guinness World Records, "Best-Selling Book," Guinnessworldrecords.com, accessed February 19, 2020, https://www.guinnessworldrecords.com/world-records/best-selling-book-of-non-fiction/.

23. Jeff Goodell, "Steve Jobs in 1994: The Rolling Stone Interview," *Rolling Stone*, January 17, 2011, https://www.rollingstone.com/culture/culture-news/steve-jobs-in-1994-the-rolling-stone-interview-231132/.

24 Mike Berardino, "Mike Tyson Explains One of His Most Famous Quotes," *South Florida Sun Sentinel*, November 9, 2012, https://www.sun-sentinel.com/sports/fl-xpm-2012-11-09-sfl-mike-tyson-explains-one-of-his-most-famous-quotes-20121109-story.html.

25 The Jane Goodall Institute, "Pledge to Eat Less Meat," Janegoodall.org, accessed February 14, 2020, http://team.janegoodall.org/site/PageServer?pagename=ieatmeatless_pledge.

26 Belinda Luscombe, "Do We Need $75,000 a Year to Be Happy?" *Time*, September 6, 2010, https://content.time.com/time/magazine/article/0,9171,2019628,00.html

About the Author

As a senior partner, the vice president of recruiting, and an executive-level sales and leadership coach for Southwestern Consulting, Ron Alford is an expert in recruiting, sales training, and coaching, helping individuals and teams to reach higher than they ever imagined. Alford has shattered every sales and revenue record at Southwestern Consulting since joining the company in 2013. He was the fastest person to reach the senior partner level in Southwestern Consulting company history. He is a company record holder with Southwestern Advantage, having personally achieved the highest level of sales seventy times. He's also a leadership record holder, coaching and training more top 1 percent producers than any other manager since Southwestern Advantage was founded in 1868. Most of all, Alford is a devoted dad and husband, all while continuing to push the distance in his trail-ultrarunning endeavors.

HAVE RON SPEAK AT YOUR NEXT EVENT!

For more on having Ron speak at your next conference or sales meeting, contact Southwestern Speakers: **SouthwesternConsulting.com/speakers**

At Southwestern Speakers, we understand what it takes to inspire and move an audience. Our speakers set the bar high for dynamic keynotes on sales, leadership, motivation and productivity. Our team will help you find the right speaker for your event who will meet your needs and your budget. We'll guide you through the booking process and answer any questions you may have along the way!

CHECK OUT OTHER GREAT TITLES FROM SOUTHWESTERN

From overcoming belief barriers and obstacles, to goal-setting, positive self-talk or navigating different personality types, visit **SouthwesternBooks.com**. We wrote the book on all things sales, leadership and entrepreneurship!

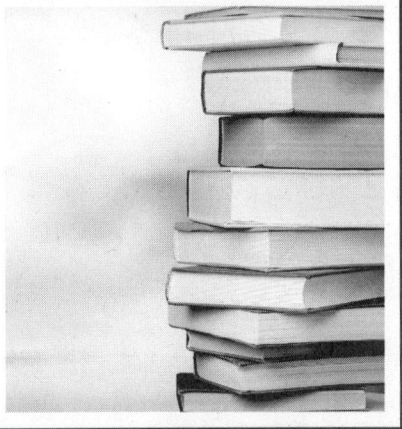

HOW DOES COACHING WORK?

Our 12-month Southwestern Coaching program provides tools, resources, and training as part of our proven coaching curriculum to help deliver measurable success over time. In addition, individuals are paired with a coach who helps outline their goals and provides accountability through 1:1 calls each month.

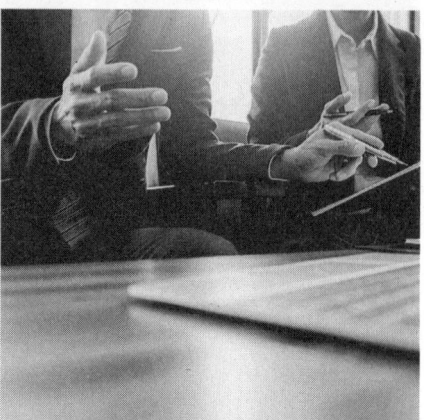

WANT TO TAKE YOUR SKILLS TO THE NEXT LEVEL?

Ever wish you could have a coach like Ron in your corner? The world of sales and leadership can be tough, and even the best need a little help from time to time!

Get a free consultation from a sales and leadership coach on Ron's team, Southwestern Consulting. We'll help understand your current situation, including your goals, unique obstacles and long-term vision. What is the cost of standing still? What are the unique goals you want to reach? Our professional coaches can help outline a plan to get you from where you are to where you want to be.

GET A FREE CONSULTATION!